The Strange Case of Dr Jekyll and Mr Hyde

GCSE English Literature for AQA

Student Book

Caroline Woolfe

Series editor: Peter Thomas

CAMBRIDGE
UNIVERSITY PRESS

University Printing House, Cambridge CB2 8BS, United Kingdom

Cambridge University Press is part of the University of Cambridge.

It furthers the University's mission by disseminating knowledge in the pursuit of education, learning and research at the highest international levels of excellence.

www.cambridge.org
Information on this title: www.cambridge.org/ukschools/9781107454224 (Paperback)
www.cambridge.org/ukschools/9781107454248 (Cambridge Elevate-enhanced Edition)
www.cambridge.org/ukschools/9781107454279 (Paperback + Cambridge Elevate-enhanced Edition)

© Cambridge University Press 2015

First published 2015

Printed in the United Kingdom by Latimer Trend

A catalogue record for this publication is available from the British Library

ISBN 978-1-107-45422-4 Paperback
ISBN 978-1-107-45424-8 Cambridge Elevate-enhanced Edition
ISBN 978-1-107-45427-9 Paperback + Cambridge Elevate-enhanced Edition

Additional resources for this publication at www.cambridge.org/ukschools

Cambridge University Press has no responsibility for the persistence or accuracy of URLs for external or third-party internet websites referred to in this publication, and does not guarantee that any content on such websites is, or will remain, accurate or appropriate. Information regarding prices, travel timetables, and other factual information given in this work is correct at the time of first printing but Cambridge University Press does not guarantee the accuracy of such information thereafter.

Message from AQA

This textbook has been approved by AQA for use with our qualification. This means that we have checked that it broadly covers the specification and we are satisfied with the overall quality. Full details of our approval process can be found on our website.

We approve textbooks because we know how important it is for teachers and students to have the right resources to support their teaching and learning. However, the publisher is ultimately responsible for the editorial control and quality of this book.

Please note that when teaching the GCSE English Literature (8702) course, you must refer to AQA's specification as your definitive source of information. While this book has been written to match the specification, it cannot provide complete coverage of every aspect of the course.

A wide range of other useful resources can be found on the relevant subject pages of our website: www.aqa.org.uk

Contents

Introduction

Welcome to your GCSE English Literature for AQA student book on *The Strange Case of Dr Jekyll and Mr Hyde*. This is one of Robert Louis Stevenson's best-known novels, and we hope you will enjoy it both as you study it for GCSE and later in life.

The story is famous for the mystery and horror that it creates around the identity of its main character. As well as being a gripping account of strange events and scientific discovery, the novel will make you think about big ideas such as good and evil and the truth about human nature. This student book will help you make the most of the novel and of your GCSE. It will develop your skills in reading and responding to a 19th-century novel, and in writing for GCSE English Literature.

Part 1: Exploring the novel

Part 1 leads you through the ten chapters of *The Strange Case of Dr Jekyll and Mr Hyde*. It ensures that you build a thorough understanding of the plot, structure and methods that Stevenson used to create a popular and entertaining novel for his readers in 1886 – one that has been enjoyed for the last 130 years.

Each unit provides text-based activities, as well as questions for discussion and other types of activity. Links to digital footage on Cambridge Elevate will deepen your experience, understanding, interpretations and analysis of the novel. You will also develop your skills in writing about the novel. Your work with each unit will result in notes and focused responses on aspects that are important for GCSE. These will also be useful when you revise for your exam.

Part 2: The novel as a whole

Part 2 provides an overview of key aspects of *The Strange Case of Dr Jekyll and Mr Hyde*, including structure, characterisation, language, themes and contexts. It will develop your detailed knowledge and understanding, and also help you to revise your responses to the novel as a whole.

Preparing for your exam

This part of this book gives you practice and guidance to help you prepare for your examination. It provides examples of answers showing skills at different levels, so you can assess where your skills are strong and where to focus your efforts to improve.

We hope that you will enjoy using these resources, not only to support your GCSE English Literature study, but also to help you see that 19th-century novels have plenty to say about the life around you – and within you.

Peter Thomas
Series Editor

Introducing
The Strange Case of Dr Jekyll and Mr Hyde

THE 19TH-CENTURY NOVEL AND
THE STRANGE CASE OF DR JEKYLL
AND MR HYDE

The 19th-century novel

Stevenson wrote in an age long before TV and digital media, when cheap printing made books and magazines available to increasing numbers of people. It was a period of growth in the publishing of fiction, when the works of authors such as Jane Austen, the Brontë sisters, Walter Scott and Charles Dickens were very popular. Readers enjoyed stories of romance and adventure, as well as novels that reflected the concerns of people's lives in the changing world of the 19th century.

There was a real appetite for horror and ghost stories, which gave readers a thrill of terror – especially at Christmas or in the dark winter evenings. Some of the books written for this market were known as 'shilling shockers': cheaply produced books costing just a shilling, which people could share at home. Stevenson wrote *The Strange Case of Dr Jekyll and Mr Hyde* late in 1885, intending it for publication at Christmas. However, delays meant that it did not appear until 1886.

Stevenson the writer

Robert Louis Stevenson was born in Edinburgh in 1850, although he later moved away from Scotland because its climate was not good for his health. He had a lifelong interest in writing and, from an early age, he was determined to make his living as a writer. At first he wrote travel articles for magazines, based on his experiences in different countries; later he published books about his journeys. He was a keen traveller who made some adventurous trips on his own. For example he described a journey around northern France by canoe, and later wrote a book about hiking in the remote hills of south-central France accompanied only by a donkey.

He became well known as a writer after the publication of his children's adventure story *Treasure Island* in 1883, but even this did not make him enough money to live independently. He wrote *The Strange Case of Dr Jekyll and Mr Hyde* in the hope that it would bring financial success – and it did. It was immediately popular, and was soon adapted into a stage play. Stevenson went on to write several other popular novels, and continued writing until his death in Samoa in 1896.

THE 19TH-CENTURY NOVEL AND GCSE ENGLISH LITERATURE

Your GCSE English Literature course has been designed to include a range of drama, prose and poetry texts from the last few hundred years. *The Strange Case of Dr Jekyll and Mr Hyde* is a novella (a short novel) – one we hope you will find interesting and rewarding to study.

At the end of your GCSE course in English Literature, you will sit an exam. This is made up of two papers:

- **Paper 1:** Shakespeare and the 19th-century novel. This is worth 40% of your GCSE English Literature.
- **Paper 2:** Modern texts and poetry. This is worth 60% of your GCSE English Literature.

There are two sections in Paper 1:

- **Section A: Shakespeare.** You will answer one question on the play you have studied. You will be required to write in detail about an extract from the play and then to write about the play as a whole.
- **Section B: The19th-century novel.** You will answer one question on the novel you have studied – *The Strange Case of Dr Jekyll and Mr Hyde* in this case. You will be required to write in detail about an extract from the novel and then to write about the novel as a whole.

GCSE ENGLISH LITERATURE ASSESSMENT OBJECTIVES

The assessment objectives (AOs) form the basis for the GCSE English Literature mark scheme. Your answer in Paper 1, Section B (the 19th-century novel) will be read by an examiner, who will be guided by these three assessment objectives:

AO1: Read, understand and respond to texts. Students should be able to:

- maintain a critical style and develop an informed personal response
- use textual references, including quotations, to support and illustrate interpretations.

AO2: Analyse the language, form and structure used by a writer to create meanings and effects, using relevant subject terminology where appropriate.

AO3: Show understanding of the relationships between texts and the contexts in which they were written.

 Learning checkpoint

The assessment objectives mean that in your GCSE English Literature exams you need to show that you:

✔ understand what has been written
✔ have formed opinions about the book and are able to express them
✔ understand how the language makes things seem real, interesting or frightening
✔ have something to say about the form the writing takes and how it is structured
✔ have some sense of context for the events in the book, the time it was written and how it may be relevant today
✔ can support your arguments and opinions by quoting the novel itself.

'I purchased at once, from a firm of wholesale chemists, a large quantity of a particular salt which I knew, from my experiments, to be the last ingredient required.'

Jekyll: Chapter 10

LITERATURE SKILLS

Most of the skills you develop in your literature study will be the same as those that you need in your GCSE English Language for reading. Using this book, you will develop your core skills to show **understanding**, **interpretation** and **analysis** of the novel. The activities in it will help you to develop your written response to be convincing in your critical explorations of the novel and the questions you are asked about it.

What these terms mean for you

At a simple level, showing **understanding** means being able to explain what happens in the story and how characters behave. However, it really needs more than this: you need to show you have understood that the way in which Stevenson wrote the story has shaped its meaning. This book will help you to identify and understand the ideas that the novel deals with and give your personal response to them. You will see that these ideas are important to the characters Stevenson created, as well as to readers of the novel – both in the 19th century and in the modern day.

Your **interpretation** is the conclusion that you reach through careful consideration of the story, its ideas and Stevenson's methods of writing it. The activities in this book will help you develop your interpretation by focusing on details and getting you to explore ways of thinking about them. As you become familiar with the novel, you should feel confident about giving your interpretation and be able to support your views with details from the text.

An interesting approach to literature study is the **analysis** of the methods that writers use in their works. It is like exploring how a film or music video has been put together to make it successful with an audience.

The first thing to remember is that Stevenson chose how to tell his story. It is all made up, and he put in the characters, descriptions and events in order to create particular effects for his readers. Today, 130 years later, you will be able to judge how the choices he made affect your reaction to the characters, your attitude towards the events, your opinions about the big ideas he explores. You will learn about aspects of language, form and structure to give you the tools to analyse the novel in a literary way.

Using details from the text

You do not have to learn long quotations off by heart. In fact, the best answers are usually ones that contain short, carefully selected quotations of just a few words. The activities in this book will help you become familiar with the novel so that you can use key words and phrases confidently as evidence for your discussion and answers. When you examine characters, for example, you will find that Stevenson himself often sums up what you need to know in a few words or a memorable phrase. Make sure that you have something to say about the quotations – perhaps explaining a feature of the language Stevenson uses, or commenting on the ideas and impressions that his words convey.

'You are sure he used a key?'

Utterson: Chapter 1

Preparing for an extract-based exam

This book will help you to work confidently with short passages from the novel and make links with the novel as a whole. In the exam, you will be given an extract as a starting point for you to answer a question, so the activities here are designed to help you to build your notes with connections and comparisons. Whenever you read part of the novel, practise by asking yourself these questions:

- How does it fit in the story?
- Which characters appear and how are they presented?
- What ideas or themes does it cover?
- How does the writer's language make it interesting or mysterious or horrifying, or something else?
- Where else in the novel have you noticed similar details?

Beyond the exam

Your GCSE English Literature is the main focus as you start to study the novel, but it does not have to be the only reason to read 19th-century literature. If you enjoy *The Strange Case of Dr Jekyll and Mr Hyde*, you may like other mystery stories written during this period. For example Arthur Conan Doyle published his Sherlock Holmes detective stories around this time. If Stevenson's novel gives you a taste for horror, you might be interested to learn more about the gothic tradition in Part 2 of this book. If you would like to read some gothic horror, try *Frankenstein* by Mary Shelley or look at the way in which Jane Austen mocks readers' fears of chilling stories in *Northanger Abbey*.

Whatever you read next, you will find that what you have learnt from your study of *The Strange Case of Dr Jekyll and Mr Hyde* will bring to it an extra level of insight and understanding. That is one of the great pleasures of English Literature. We hope you enjoy it, and we wish you luck.

'My two natures had memory in common, but all other faculties were most unequally shared between them.'

Jekyll: Chapter 10

1

Introducing a mystery

How does Stevenson set up the story?

Your progress in this unit:
- understand the characters and events introduced at the start of the novel
- explore how Stevenson presents them
- identify links between this story and other detective and mystery fiction
- explore attitudes towards respectability.

GETTING STARTED – THE STORY AND YOU

What's it all about?

Since it was first published in 1886, *The Strange Case of Dr Jekyll and Mr Hyde* has become a popular and influential story.

1 Use the internet to find some pictures of the **characters** of Jekyll and Hyde. What do these pictures tell you about the original book and the ideas in it?

2 What sort of **genre** is suggested by the images you have found?

What does being 'respectable' mean?

The Strange Case of Dr Jekyll and Mr Hyde is set in the 19th century. The characters in it are members of the middle class, which was becoming increasingly influential at the time. Most people of this class had strong Christian values and wanted to be seen as models of good behaviour. Ideas about respectability are an important **theme** in the novel.

1 Work in pairs. Each of you should think of a living person you consider to be 'respectable'. Describe this person to your partner, but do not give their name. Your partner should try to identify the person from your description. Afterwards, swap over and guess your partner's 'respectable' person.

2 What do you think makes a person respectable in the 21st century? In your pairs, agree on a description of 'respectability' and write it down. You could use some of these words in your description:

role model	reputation	status
example	social norms	decency
morality	values	

 Key terms

characters: the people in a story; even when based on real people, characters in a novel are invented or fictionalised.

genre: the kind or type of literature to which a text belongs; stories within a particular genre will have similar characteristics.

theme: an idea that a writer keeps returning to, exploring it from different perspectives.

 Watch a performance of 'Story of the door' on Cambridge Elevate.

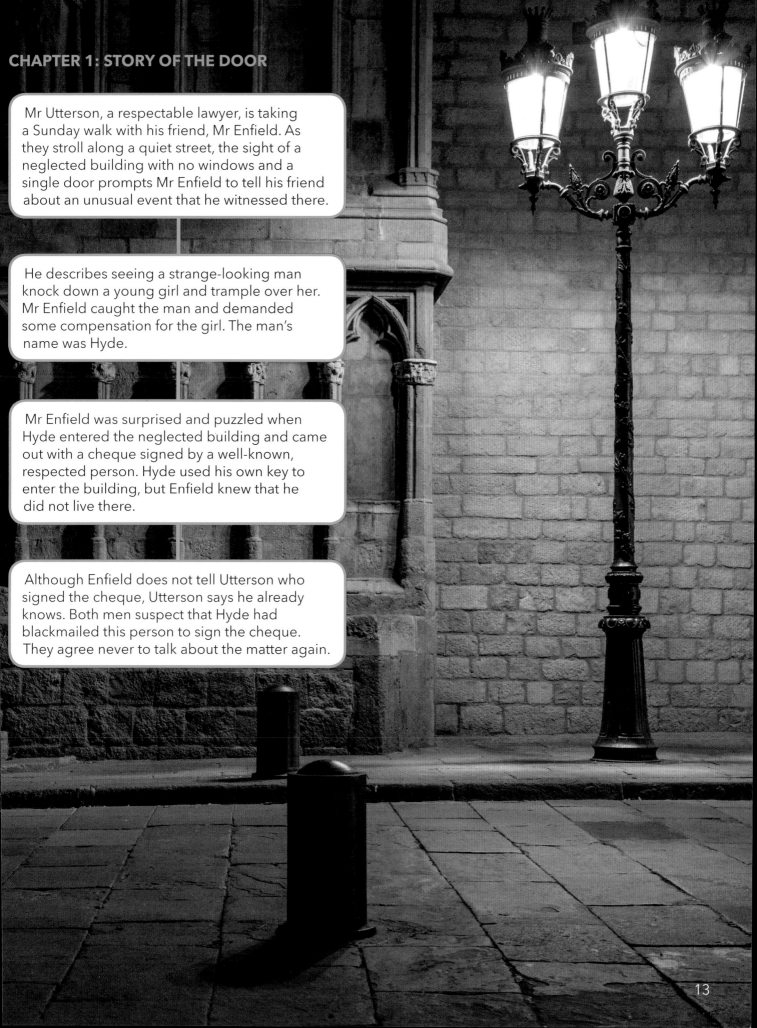

CHAPTER 1: STORY OF THE DOOR

Mr Utterson, a respectable lawyer, is taking a Sunday walk with his friend, Mr Enfield. As they stroll along a quiet street, the sight of a neglected building with no windows and a single door prompts Mr Enfield to tell his friend about an unusual event that he witnessed there.

He describes seeing a strange-looking man knock down a young girl and trample over her. Mr Enfield caught the man and demanded some compensation for the girl. The man's name was Hyde.

Mr Enfield was surprised and puzzled when Hyde entered the neglected building and came out with a cheque signed by a well-known, respected person. Hyde used his own key to enter the building, but Enfield knew that he did not live there.

Although Enfield does not tell Utterson who signed the cheque, Utterson says he already knows. Both men suspect that Hyde had blackmailed this person to sign the cheque. They agree never to talk about the matter again.

GETTING CLOSER – FOCUS ON DETAILS

Mr Enfield's testimony

Mr Enfield is a lawyer. He is Utterson's friend and **'distant kinsman, the well-known man about town'**. Enfield gives the first account of Mr Hyde when he tells Utterson about the disturbing event he witnessed. The term **testimony** is used to describe this kind of account given by a witness in a story.

1 Read Mr Enfield's account of what happened when he first saw Mr Hyde. Note down any key phrases that relate to:

 a   where the event takes place
 b   Mr Enfield's thoughts and feelings
 c   Mr Hyde's actions
 d   paying compensation.

2 Work in pairs. One of you takes on the role of Mr Enfield and gives a spoken account of what happened, using as many key phrases as possible. The other person listens, then gives feedback on the accuracy of the account. Try to identify any key points or phrases that have been missed out.

3 In your pairs, come up with two questions that need answering about each of the following parts of Enfield's story:

 a   the neglected building
 b   the door
 c   Mr Hyde
 d   the cheque.

PUTTING DETAILS TO USE

Understanding Mr Utterson

Stevenson introduces the character of Mr Utterson in the opening lines of the novel. He describes him as **'the last reputable acquaintance and the last good influence in the lives of down-going men'**. What do you think the words **'reputable'** and **'good'** and the phrase **'the lives of down-going men'** suggest about Utterson's qualities?

1 Look at the following descriptions of Utterson's character. For each one, decide whether the language reflects Utterson's profession as a lawyer or whether it suggests something about his personality.

 a   cold
 b   dreary
 c   austere
 d   lovable
 e   eminently human
 f   tolerance for others
 g   dusty
 h   inclined to help rather than to reprove.

Enfield's and Utterson's attitudes

Enfield and Utterson believe that Hyde is blackmailing someone. Knowing how easy it is to destroy someone's good reputation and respectability, Enfield does not name the person who signed the cheque. Stevenson may be suggesting that even this 'respectable' person could have something to hide – and that these two lawyers are turning a blind eye to it:

I incline to Cain's heresy [...] I let my brother go to the devil in his own way.

Utterson: Chapter 1

In the Bible, Cain killed his brother Abel. When God asked Cain where Abel was, he replied, 'Am I my brother's keeper?' Utterson calls this **'heresy'** because it goes against the Christian teaching of love for others.

 Contexts

In the late 19th century, the law was a wealthy profession and lawyers enjoyed high status in society. They were valued for their role in the important business of property ownership, inheritance and legal disputes. They had to be trustworthy and discreet in the way they dealt with people who might be on the right or the wrong side of the law.

1 Enfield explains himself in more detail later on in the chapter. See if you can find the passage. Here are some words and phrases to help you:

a The '**day of judgement**' is a reference to passages in the Bible that describe how God will judge the dead according to what they have done in their lives.

b To be in '**Queer Street**' means to be in financial or other difficulties.

2 Both Utterson and Enfield seem reluctant to go into detail about Mr Hyde. Read the text again and identify which of the two characters says each of the following quotations.

a 'signed with a name I can't mention'
b 'that's a good rule of yours'
c 'Here is another lesson to say nothing.'
d 'Let us make a bargain never to refer to this again.'

Watch actors and the director discuss the characters of Utterson and Enfield on Cambridge Elevate.

Learning checkpoint

Use the activity in the section 'Understanding Mr Utterson' to help you write a short paragraph summarising your impressions of Mr Utterson's character in Chapter 1.

How will I know I've done this well?

✔ **The best answers** will explore why Stevenson wanted to show different sides to a character, and analyse the way he uses language to make his reader understand Utterson. They will offer a personal response and include supportive details from the text.

✔ **Good answers** will explain how Stevenson has made Utterson's character interesting and believable in the story. They will include references to some well-chosen details.

✔ **Weaker answers** will describe Utterson as a real person and what he does in the story as if it were true. It will not include many examples or mention what Stevenson does as a writer.

Key terms

testimony: an account given by a witness to an event.

... the last reputable acquaintance and the last good influence in the lives of down-going men.

Chapter 1

3 Look at the following statements about the attitudes of Enfield and Utterson. Decide whether you agree or disagree with each one, or whether you can't yet say. Find quotations from the text to support your answers.

a The two men show the discretion expected of lawyers and avoid gossip.

b They do not ask questions because they do not care about anybody else.

c They do not criticise others because they have secrets of their own to hide.

d They do not want to admit their suspicions about someone they know and respect.

e They avoid looking below the surface because they are afraid of what they might find.

f They want to protect the respectable reputation of someone they know.

4 Work in pairs. Write one paragraph each about Utterson. One of you should give a positive view of this character, the other a less flattering opinion. Afterwards, discuss how successfully you think you have expressed your ideas.

Choosing names

Writers carefully construct their characters to fit the stories they write. Sometimes the names a writer chooses give clues about the characters.

1 Mr Hyde's name is a **homophone**. Do you think his name is a good choice for a character in a mystery novel? Why, or why not? Consider the following:

a What associations does the word have?

b Does it suggest a good or bad character?

Find out more about character and characterisation in the novel in Unit 13.

The setting of Chapter 1

The **setting** can influence a reader's understanding and responses to a story. Read the description of the street and building that prompt Mr Enfield to tell his tale (beginning '**It chanced on one of these rambles**'). Now look at this example of a student's analysis of Stevenson's language:

---

*Stevenson describes a busy street in London. During the week it is a shopping street. Stevenson describes the shop fronts as being inviting, 'like rows of smiling saleswomen'. This **simile** brings the shops alive, making them seem welcoming to customers. He creates a contrast between this street and the 'dingy neighbourhood' around it.*

Opening sentences give an interpretation of the scene.
Focus on a short quotation embedded in a sentence ready for analysis.
Uses literary term to describe the language and comment on its effect.

Do you agree with the student's interpretation? Before you do Activity 1, think about whether there are any points that you would add or change to improve the analysis.

1 Read the next paragraph, which focuses on '**a certain sinister block of building**'. Using the example as a model, write an analysis of this paragraph. Think about how the **adjectives** ('**sinister**', '**blind**', '**discoloured**', '**sordid**', '**blistered**', '**distained**') might create an impression of the building or **contrast** it with the street on which it stands.

Find out more about context and setting in the novel in Unit 12.

GETTING IT INTO WRITING

How does Stevenson engage the reader?

 Write a paragraph explaining how Stevenson engages the reader's interest in some mysterious events in Chapter 1.

2 Write a paragraph explaining how Stevenson presents Mr Utterson. Do you think he comes across as an important character? Why, or why not? What evidence can you find to suggest that he might be capable of investigating the mysteries?

3 Swap your paragraphs with a partner. Talk about how well you have understood details from the text and explained Stevenson's presentation.

Complete this assignment on Cambridge Elevate.

GETTING FURTHER

Ideas about duality

Chapter 1 introduces the theme of duality – the idea that there are two aspects or ways of seeing things.

1 Copy and complete the following table to identify how Stevenson presents the theme of duality through the characters and settings in Chapter 1. Include your own comments and short quotations from the text. Some examples have been given to start you off.

 Key terms

homophone: a word that sounds the same as another word, but which has a different spelling and meaning, e.g. Hyde/hide.

setting: the description of the place in which a story is set.

simile: a comparison between two things that uses the words 'as' or 'like'.

adjective: a word that describes a person, place or thing.

contrast: to point out the ways in which two or more things are different from one another.

	On one hand …	On the other hand …
Mr Utterson	Unfriendly and cold? 'never lighted by a smile' 'backward in sentiment'	Tolerant and helps others? 'eminently human' 'somehow lovable'
the street		It shines out in contrast to its neighbours.
the man who signed the cheque for Mr Hyde	He was woken up to give money willingly to the unpleasant and 'detestable' Mr Hyde.	
the building with the door		Somebody must live there because Enfield says there is …

2

The investigation begins

How do the characters and the mystery develop?

GETTING STARTED – THE STORY AND YOU

Friendships under strain

1 Briefly make notes on what you would do if you found yourself in the following situations with a close friend.

a   You are worried that your friend has got in with the wrong crowd, but they won't listen when you try to talk to them about it.

b   You suspect that your friend is hiding an embarrassing secret from their past.

c   You are concerned that a dangerous person seems to have some kind of hold over your friend.

2 Work in pairs and compare the notes you made. In what ways are your reactions the same? In what ways are they different?

 Watch a summary of 'Search for Mr Hyde' on Cambridge Elevate.

Inheritance

A will sets out what a person wants to happen to their money, property and possessions after their death. It is a legal document, so a copy is usually left with a lawyer who sorts things out when the person dies. A person named to receive something in a will is called a 'beneficiary'.

1 Copy the following spider diagram, then add any other reasons you can think of why someone might be named as a beneficiary in a will. There may be good or bad reasons.

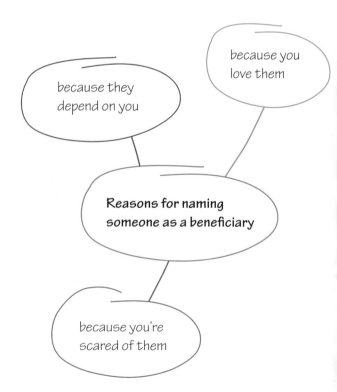

because you love them

because they depend on you

Reasons for naming someone as a beneficiary

because you're scared of them

Utterson knows that the person who signed the cheque for Hyde is his friend, Dr Jekyll. Utterson reads Jekyll's will and discovers that Hyde is named as a beneficiary. Utterson is puzzled about Jekyll's relationship with Hyde because the will states that Hyde should inherit the property not just if Jekyll dies, but also in the case of his '**disappearance or unexplained absence**'.

Utterson is afraid that Hyde has some power over Jekyll, perhaps because Jekyll is hiding a shameful secret. Utterson decides to find out more about Hyde.

Utterson visits Dr Lanyon, who explains that he and Jekyll are no longer friends – they had a disagreement about Jekyll's unscientific ideas. Lanyon knows nothing about Hyde.

The next day, after having a terrible nightmare about Hyde, Utterson keeps watch near the door that Hyde used to gain access to Jekyll's house. Eventually, he sees Hyde approaching. They talk briefly, and Hyde gives Utterson his address in a different part of London.

Utterson walks around the corner to the main entrance to Dr Jekyll's house. The butler tells him that Jekyll is out and that Hyde is free to come and go through the back door using his own key.

GETTING CLOSER – FOCUS ON DETAILS

Interpreting Utterson's language

In Chapter 2, Utterson expresses his thoughts about Jekyll and considers why Hyde may be able to blackmail him:

> … <u>he is in deep waters</u>! He was wild when he was young; a long while ago to be sure; but in the law of God, there is no statute of limitations. Ay, it must be that; <u>the ghost of some old sin</u>, <u>the cancer of some concealed disgrace</u>.

Utterson: Chapter 2

1 The **metaphor** 'he is in deep waters' suggests that Jekyll is in trouble by creating the impression that he is in danger of drowning. What do you think the two other underlined metaphors suggest about the way Jekyll's past behaviour might be affecting him now?

Read the following quotations relating to Jekyll's will. The annotations explain the ideas that Stevenson conveys in them. Do you agree with the annotations, or do you have a different opinion about the ideas Stevenson is conveying?

> … his 'friend and benefactor, Edward Hyde'.

↑

The beneficiary of the will seems to be someone Jekyll regards highly.

> This document had long been the lawyer's eyesore.

↑

Utterson has been troubled by the will for a long time.

 Find out more about language in the novel in Unit 15.

2 Read the first paragraph of Chapter 2 again. In pairs, talk about why the following details and quotations might be significant.

a The will is '**holographic**' (handwritten).
b '**disappearance or unexplained absence for any period exceeding three calendar months**'
c '**the name was but a name of which he could learn no more**'
d '**out of the shifting, insubstantial mists that had so long baffled his eye there leaped up the sudden, definite presentment of a fiend.**'

 Watch an adaptation of Utterson and Jekyll discussing the will on Cambridge Elevate.

PUTTING DETAILS TO USE

Utterson as investigator

Stevenson uses the **character** of Utterson to guide the reader through the mystery. Utterson sets about his investigations like a detective, and uses a **pun** to state his determination: '**If he be Mr Hyde [...] I shall be Mr Seek.**'

1 Look at this extract:

> 'Ay, I must put my shoulder to the wheel – if Jekyll will but let me,' he added, 'if Jekyll will only let me.' For once more he saw before his mind's eye, as clear as a transparency, the strange clauses of the will.

Chapter 2

a What does the phrase '**I must put my shoulder to the wheel**' suggest about Utterson? Choose a word (or think of your own) to describe how you think he is feeling about the task ahead: determined, scared, excited, bored, annoyed.
b Why do you think Utterson repeats the phrase '**If Jekyll will only let me**'?

2 Think about the way Utterson begins collecting evidence in Chapter 2.

   a Make brief notes on the questions he asks Dr Lanyon and Jekyll's butler, Poole.

   b What information does Utterson discover from these 'witnesses'?

Look at the language Stevenson uses to describe Utterson's hunt for Mr Hyde. The highlights show you different types of analysis and interpretation.

In the morning before office hours, at noon when business was plenty and time scarce, at night under the face of the fogged city moon, by all lights and at all hours of solitude or concourse, the lawyer was to be found on his chosen post.

Chapter 2

The words in green refer to every part of the day to emphasise Utterson's dedication to his task.

The phrases in blue contain repeated words to show the repetitive nature of Utterson's surveillance.

The words in pink express contrasting ideas to show that Utterson stayed there in spite of other demands on his time.

Utterson's nightmare

The description of Utterson's nightmare reflects the **romantic** belief that imagination and emotion can overcome rational behaviour. By day, Mr Utterson is a rational lawyer, but his deep concerns about Jekyll and Hyde surface in a nightmare.

1 Read the description of Utterson's nightmare. Put all the details in a table like this, then match them to the details from Enfield's account of meeting Mr Hyde in Chapter 1.

Utterson's nightmare	Enfield's story
'field of lamps in a nocturnal city'	'street after street, all lighted up'

Utterson's dream is haunted by the ghostly figure of Hyde:

… if at any time he dozed over, it was but to see it glide more stealthily through sleeping houses, or move the more swiftly and still the more swiftly, even to dizziness, through wider labyrinths of lamplighted city, and at every street corner crush a child and leave her screaming.

Chapter 2

2 Write a short paragraph describing how the way this extract is written helps the reader to understand Utterson's dream and the effect it has on him.

Key terms

metaphor: a type of comparison that describes one thing as if it was another.

pun: a play on words; the use of a word or phrase with a double meaning.

romantic: ideas in literature based on the part that human instincts, imagination and emotions play in a person's identity.

Learning checkpoint

The figure in Utterson's dream **'had no face by which he might know it'**. Read the description (up to '... **the real features of Mr Hyde**'). Use what you have learnt so far to explain how the descripion in Utterson's nightmare builds up suspense about Hyde's face. To do this well, you should consider and explain:

✔ the use of pronouns
✔ the effects of the verbs used
✔ the structure of the passage.

The presentation of Mr Hyde

Stevenson frequently uses animal or inhuman **imagery** to describe Mr Hyde.

1 Copy and complete the following table to explain the imagery and the impression it gives of Mr Hyde. Add other examples as you read more.

Imagery	Impression
'with a hissing intake of breath'	
'snarled aloud'	
'a savage laugh'	

Night and day – light and dark

Stevenson uses contrasts between night and day to add to the atmosphere of the story.

1 Copy and complete the following table to show the effects of the **settings** of particular events in Chapters 1 and 2. An example has been done to start you off.

Event	Time of day and/or atmosphere	Effect achieved
Utterson's walk with Enfield	quiet Sunday afternoon	uneventful and innocent day of rest before the mystery starts
Enfield's encounter with Hyde		
Utterson's return home from his walk with Enfield		
Utterson's visit to Dr Lanyon		
Utterson's meeting with Hyde		

GETTING IT INTO WRITING

Writing about Stevenson's presentation of Hyde

 1 Write a short piece (about 150 words) exploring how Stevenson presents Mr Hyde's appearance and behaviour.

You should start by picking two short passages from the text that you can compare. What extracts do you think would be useful for you to use here? Think about any points so far where Hyde has been described.

In your writing you should:

- compare the two passages, focusing on their similarities and differences
- use and comment on quotations
- include some analysis of Stevenson's language choices
- explain the effects of the description.

✔ **Complete this assignment on Cambridge Elevate.**

GETTING FURTHER

The character of Dr Lanyon

Dr Lanyon reappears as an important character later in the story.

 1 Write a short paragraph commenting on the effect of the **adjectives** in this description of Dr Lanyon's appearance:

> This was a hearty, healthy, dapper, red-faced gentleman, with a shock of hair prematurely white, and a boisterous and decided manner.

Chapter 2

2 Write a short paragraph about the impression Stevenson gives of Dr Lanyon in his description of how Lanyon greets Utterson

🔑 **Key terms**

imagery: language intended to conjure up a vivid picture in the reader's mind.

Mr Hyde was pale and dwarfish, he gave an impression of deformity without any nameable malformation.

Chapter 2

3

Meeting Dr Jekyll

How does Stevenson present Dr Jekyll?

Your progress in this unit:

- understand Stevenson's presentation of Dr Jekyll
- understand Utterson's relationship with Jekyll
- examine how the author uses dialogue to tell the story
- make links with what you have learnt about the novel so far.

GETTING STARTED – THE STORY AND YOU

What do you expect of Dr Jekyll?

Stevenson delays introducing the **character** of Dr Jekyll until Chapter 3. This is the first time the reader finds out how he looks, speaks and behaves.

1 Work in pairs. Make notes on everything you know about Dr Jekyll from the story so far. Then draw up a table with the following headings and put each piece of information in the appropriate column.

   a Facts
   b Other characters' opinions and feelings about him
   c Your own response and predictions.

2 In the title of the novel Dr Jekyll is named first, yet Mr Hyde appears in the story before Dr Jekyll. In your pairs, talk about the effect you think delaying Jekyll's introduction has on the story.

GETTING CLOSER – FOCUS ON DETAILS

Read the summary. Then read Chapter 3.

Utterson – a good friend

The discreet and tolerant Mr Utterson seems to be a good friend – people '**liked to sit awhile in his unobtrusive company**'.

1 In this section, Stevenson **contrasts** Utterson with other people in order to describe his character. List the words Stevenson uses to make this contrast.

PUTTING DETAILS TO USE

The presentation of Dr Jekyll

Look at how Stevenson describes Dr Jekyll:

… a large, well-made, smooth-faced man of fifty, with something of a slyish cast perhaps, but every mark of capacity and kindness — you could see by his looks that he cherished for Mr Utterson a sincere and warm affection.

Chapter 3

Watch Robert Louis Stevenson discuss his presentation of Dr Jekyll on Cambridge Elevate.

Dr Jekyll hosts a dinner party for a group of friends, including Mr Utterson.

When the others have left at the end of the evening, Utterson takes the opportunity to speak to Dr Jekyll about his will.

Jekyll tries to change the subject, but Utterson persists. He tells Jekyll he is concerned because he has heard bad things about Mr Hyde. Utterson invites Jekyll to explain the situation so that he can help him.

Although Jekyll says that he trusts Utterson more than anyone else, he refuses to give more information. Instead, he asks Utterson to keep the matter private and makes him promise to carry out the instructions in his will if he should disappear.

1 Identify the words and phrases in the first paragraph of Chapter 3 that seem to create a good impression of Jekyll.

2 Re-read the description of Mr Hyde from Chapter 2. Write a paragraph noting the physical differences between Dr Jekyll and Mr Hyde based on these two descriptions. You may find the following words and phrases useful when writing about contrasts:

whereas	however
in contrast	unlike Dr Jekyll, Mr Hyde is …

Stevenson's use of dialogue

After the opening paragraph, the whole of Chapter 3 is written as **dialogue**. Writers often use this technique to reveal more about the characters and to make them seem realistic.

1 Copy and complete the following table to show what you think the different features of the dialogue reveal about the characters.

Features of dialogue	Examples	What this might show about the characters
words and phrases that explain how the characters speak and act during the conversation	'the doctor carried it off gaily'	Jekyll covers up his reluctance to talk about his will by answering light-heartedly and trying to change the subject.
	'with a certain incoherency of manner'	
repetition or hesitation	'this is very good of you, this is downright good of you'	

2 Find more examples of dialogue features and add them to your table.

Comparing sections of dialogue

In Chapter 2, we learn that Dr Lanyon thinks Dr Jekyll has become **'too fanciful'** and has begun to **'go wrong, wrong in mind'**. In Chapter 3, we see Jekyll's point of view:

I never saw a man so distressed as you were by my will; unless it were that hide-bound pedant, Lanyon, at what he called my scientific heresies.

Chapter 3

1 Work in pairs. Compare these two accounts of why Dr Lanyon and Dr Jekyll have drifted apart. Make notes of the reasons they each give for the breakdown of their friendship.

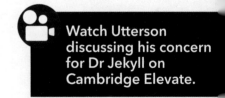

Watch Utterson discussing his concern for Dr Jekyll on Cambridge Elevate.

GETTING IT INTO WRITING

Writing from different points of view

 Imagine you are Dr Jekyll at the end of the evening of the dinner party. Utterson has just left. Write a diary entry in which you reflect on the conversation you have just had with him. What do you think of his behaviour?

 Write a similar diary entry from Utterson's point of view.

GETTING FURTHER

True or false?

 Look at the following statements. Based on the conversation between Utterson and Jekyll in Chapter 3, decide whether you think they are true or false. Give reasons for your answers.

- a   Jekyll is glad to speak privately to his old friend Utterson.
- b   Jekyll is happy to discuss his will again.
- c   Jekyll wants to stay friends with Lanyon but finds his old-fashioned views frustrating.
- d   Utterson is determined not to let Jekyll change the subject.
- e   There is no sign that Jekyll minds talking about Hyde.
- f   Utterson sincerely wants to help Jekyll if he can.
- g   Jekyll does not trust Utterson.
- h   Utterson is reluctant to help Mr Hyde.

✔ **Complete this assignment on Cambridge Elevate.**

🔑 **Key terms**

dialogue: a conversation between two or more people in a piece of writing.

✔ **Learning checkpoint**

How will I know I've done this well?

- ✔ **The best answers** will make an informed personal response using evidence from the text to support their interpretations. They will analyse how Stevenson's language shapes the reader's understanding of the conversation between Utterson and Jekyll.
- ✔ **Good answers** will show a clear understanding of the characters' points of view and how Stevenson presents them. They will use some appropriate examples from the text to support the points they make.
- ✔ **Weaker answers** will comment on the two characters, perhaps without full understanding of their points of view. They will not mention Stevenson and may have written about Utterson and Jekyll as if they were real people.

a large, well-made, smooth-faced man of fifty, with something of a slyish cast perhaps, but every mark of capacity and kindness.

Chapter 3

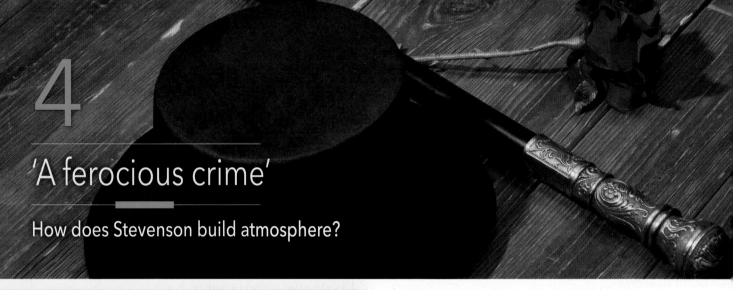

4

'A ferocious crime'

How does Stevenson build atmosphere?

Your progress in this unit:

- understand events and clues unfolding in the story
- identify Stevenson's use of contrast and explain its effects
- explore how Stevenson's presentation influences the reader's response to the characters
- consider ideas about the London setting.

GETTING STARTED – THE STORY AND YOU

Reporting criminals and victims

The Victorian public enjoyed sensational news stories as much as people do today. Crime rates were high in London in Stevenson's time, and newspapers frequently carried front-page stories of gruesome murders.

1 Work in pairs. Write a list of TV programmes about murder (for example *Midsomer Murders*, *CSI*, *Silent Witness*). Discuss why you think this is such a popular subject.

2 Work in small groups. Using newspapers and the internet, find five news stories about different crimes.

    a Discuss how the headlines makes the events seem dramatic or interesting.

    b Discuss how the reports present the victims and make you feel sorry for them.

GETTING CLOSER – FOCUS ON DETAILS

Read the summary. Then read Chapter 4.

Responses to murder

There are three **characters** at the murder scene: Mr Hyde (the murderer), Sir Danvers Carew (the victim) and the maidservant (the witness).

1 Look at the following quotations from this chapter. Identify the character to which each one applies.

    a **at peace with all men**
    b **very small gentleman**
    c **streaming tears**
    d **innocent and old-world**
    e **kindness**
    f **white hair**.

2 Explain the effect of each quotation. Use these sentence starters for help:

    a Stevenson's words make the maidservant seem …
    b Stevenson's words make Sir Danvers Carew seem …
    c Stevenson's words make Mr Hyde seem …

 Watch the maidservant describe what she saw on Cambridge Elevate.

A year later, a man called Sir Danvers Carew is murdered in London. A maidservant witnesses the crime and identifies the murderer as Mr Hyde.

The maid describes how Hyde attacked his victim with a heavy cane for no apparent reason then ran off, leaving the dead man in the lane with the broken half of the murder weapon beside him.

In his pocket, the victim had a letter addressed to Mr Utterson. Utterson identifies the body and then, hearing the maid's description of the murderer, leads the police inspector investigating the case to Hyde's home. Hyde's housekeeper says her master is not at home, and is rarely there.

Hyde's room is well-furnished and luxurious, but it has been ransacked – as if someone has been through things hurriedly. There are ashes in the fire where papers have been burned. Among them, the inspector finds the remains of a cheque book. The other half of the murder weapon is behind the door. He discovers that Hyde's bank account contains several thousand pounds.

The inspector plans to wait at the bank and arrest Hyde, but this might be difficult because he has no clear description of him. All he knows is that other people describe him as creating a sense of deformity.

PUTTING DETAILS TO USE

Stevenson's mystery trail

In Chapter 4, the police are involved for the first time. The Inspector from Scotland Yard seems pleased to discover information that will lead to the arrest of the murderer.

1 Are the following statements true or false? Find details in the text to support your answer.

    a The murderer has been positively identified as Mr Hyde.
    b The murder took place in broad daylight.
    c The motive for the murder was robbery.
    d The murder weapon has a link to Dr Jekyll.
    e The murder weapon has no link to Mr Hyde.
    f There are signs that Hyde has run away.
    g The police inspector will recognise Hyde when he sees him.

Setting and atmosphere

In this chapter, Stevenson describes the London fog during Utterson's journey to Soho. What atmosphere do you think is created by Stevenson's use of the fog? Look at the definition of **figuratively**. How might Stevenson be using the fog figuratively? Think about Utterson's state of mind as he makes his journey.

Watch a film director and location scout discuss the Soho set on Cambridge Eleva

---

A great chocolate-coloured pall lowered over heaven, but the wind was continually charging and routing these embattled vapours [...] for a moment, the fog would be quite broken up, and a haggard shaft of daylight would glance in between the swirling wreaths.

Chapter 4

---

1 Sketch your impression of the scene. Add brief quotations from the text as notes to your sketch. Then, in small groups, compare your drawings and discuss the impressions that the scene creates.

2 Read the description of the location of Hyde's house in the paragraph that starts: '**As the cab drew up**'.

    a What do the **adjectives** '**dingy**', '**low**', '**ragged**', '**blackguardly**' describe?
    b What impression do you feel they create of this **setting**?
    c Find at least two other details from this paragraph that support your interpretation.

 Find out more about context and setting in the novel in Unit 12.

Contexts

Fog was a big problem in 19th-century London, and smoke and pollution from coal fires made things worse. The result was a dismal brown smog that hung over the city – so dense that people often had to light lamps during the day. This smog also crept into buildings and caused serious health problems. In 1873 alone, 273 people died as a result of it.

Contrasting descriptions

Stevenson ends his description of the setting with the words: '**This was the home of Henry Jekyll's favourite; of a man who was heir to a quarter of a million sterling**.'

1 Work in pairs. Discuss the contrast between the wealth implied by '**a quarter of a million sterling**' and the dismal details of the scene given earlier in the paragraph.

2 Stevenson uses the phrase '**Henry Jekyll's favourite**' instead of the simpler 'Mr Hyde'. Do you think this highlights the contrast more effectively? Why, or why not?

Stevenson creates another contrast with the external setting when he describes Hyde's rooms:

A closet was filled with wine; the plate was of silver, the napery elegant; a good picture hung upon the walls, a gift (as Utterson supposed) from Henry Jekyll, who was much of a connoisseur; and the carpets were of many plies [threads] and agreeable in colour.

3 Which words in this passage seem to create an impression of luxury?

4 By making this contrast, Stevenson may be hinting that there is something suspicious about Hyde. Do you agree with this interpretation? Why, or why not? Based on what you have learnt so far, why do you think Hyde lives in such luxury?

Key terms

figuratively: when language is used to describe or represent something – for example in a metaphor.

A closet was filled with wine; the plate was of silver, the napery elegant.

Chapter 4

Stevenson's use of irony

Stevenson chooses details to make the reader look critically at the characters and try to work out why they behave in certain ways. For example he uses **irony** to suggest that Inspector Newcomen is more concerned with his own advancement than with the tragedy of the murder, writing that the inspector's '**eye lighted up with professional ambition**'.

1 Why do you think the inspector sees the investigation into Sir Danvers Carew's murder as a career opportunity? How does this interpretation fit with what you already know about the **theme** of reputation in the novel?

2 After examining Hyde's rooms, the inspector seems confident that he can catch him. Copy the following table and find quotations from the text that support the comments about the inspector's attitude.

The inspector's attitude	Quotation
He boasts about having virtually caught the criminal.	
He assumes that the arrest will be straightforward.	
He expresses certainty to assure Mr Utterson.	
He confidently interprets the clues he has found.	
He believes that he understands Mr Hyde's attitude.	

Mr Hyde's housekeeper

1 This '**ivory-faced and silvery-haired old woman**' is not given a name. She is described as having '**an evil face, smoothed by hypocrisy; but her manners were excellent**'. Which words in this description relate to the theme of double standards and concealment?

2 The housekeeper seems pleased that Mr Hyde may be in trouble – a '**flash of odious joy**' appears on her face. The phrase '**odious joy**' is an **oxymoron**. How does this oxymoron help the reader understand the character of the housekeeper?

Key terms

irony: an extra layer of meaning in something, so a reader understands more than the characters involved.

oxymoron: a figure of speech where contradictory words are put together to create a complex effect.

GETTING IT INTO WRITING

Writing about settings

Choose two short passages from Chapters 1–4 that describe settings. Here are some examples of settings you could look for descriptions of, although there are several others you might find:

- the night-time streets of Mr Enfield's story
- Jekyll's house
- the scene of Carew's murder.

1 Use your two passages to write a short essay on Stevenson's use of settings in the novel. Use the following flow chart to help you plan and write your essay.

> Choose your two passages.

⇩

> Describe the techniques that Stevenson uses in one passage, giving evidence from the text.

⇩

> Explain the atmosphere created, using short quotations from the text.

⇩

> Do the same for the second passage.

⇩

> Explain the similarities and contrasts between the settings.

⇩

> Identify a character linked to each setting. Explain how the settings help you to understand this character.

 Complete this assignment on Cambridge Elevate.

GETTING FURTHER

What does it mean to be evil?

1 Work in pairs. Talk about what you think the words 'evil' and 'wicked' mean and how they are used today.

2 Consider the following quotations. What do you think each one shows about the characters in the novel?

- **a** The maidservant describes Hyde as '**particularly wicked-looking**'.
- **b** Mr Hyde's housekeeper '**had an evil face**'.
- **c** Utterson believes that he can read '**Satan's signature**' upon Hyde's face.
- **d** Mr Enfield describes Mr Hyde as acting '**like Satan**' when surrounded by the family of the girl he trampled.

 Learning checkpoint

Imagine that you are a police officer on the case of Mr Hyde. Prepare a report on the case so far. You should include: information about Mr Hyde and your opinion of him; details of his crime and other activities; evidence collected from other characters.

How will I know I've done this well?

✔ **The best answers** will explore ideas critically and present their views in a well-structured way. They will make good use of precise details from the text to support their interpretations, showing how Stevenson's methods of telling the story have influenced their understanding.

✔ **Good answers** will explain their comments and consider ideas by examining appropriate details from the text. They will explain or comment on the methods that the writer has used and their effects on the reader.

✔ **Weaker answers** will make simple comments and may re-tell the story. They will give some supporting details and identify deliberate choices made by the writer.

Conflicting evidence

How does Stevenson use contrasts to present ideas?

Your progress in this unit:

- understand details about the relationship between Jekyll and Hyde
- identify the clues that disturb Mr Utterson
- consider the contrasting presentation of Jekyll in Chapters 3 and 5
- explain how Stevenson uses symbolism to present ideas.

GETTING STARTED – THE STORY AND YOU

Forgery and forensics

1 Work in small groups. Choose a paragraph from Chapter 5, then each person in the group should copy it out.

    a Pass the handwritten paragraphs around the group and try to identify who has written each one.

    b Discuss the features of each person's handwriting.

2 Copy out the paragraph again, this time trying to disguise your handwriting. Compare the results. Can others still identify your writing?

GETTING CLOSER – FOCUS ON DETAILS

Read the summary. Then read Chapter 5.

Jekyll's house and laboratory

When Mr Utterson visits Dr Jekyll, he is taken to a room he has not seen before – the dissecting room of the surgeon who used to live there. Utterson feels a '**distasteful sense of strangeness**' as he passes through the room.

1 Which of the words in the word bank do you think best describe the impression created by the following quotations?

    a **once crowded with eager students and now lying gaunt and silent**
    b **the floor strewn with crates and littered with packing straw**
    c **the light falling dimly through the foggy cupola.**

disordered	deathly	secretive
neglected	foreboding	experimental
gloomy	mysterious	

Contexts

Until 1832, only the corpses of executed criminals could legally be used to study and learn about the human body. There were not enough of these, and an illegal trade in bodies developed. In 1832, the Anatomy Act changed the law, allowing doctors to dissect unclaimed corpses from hospitals, workhouses and prisons.

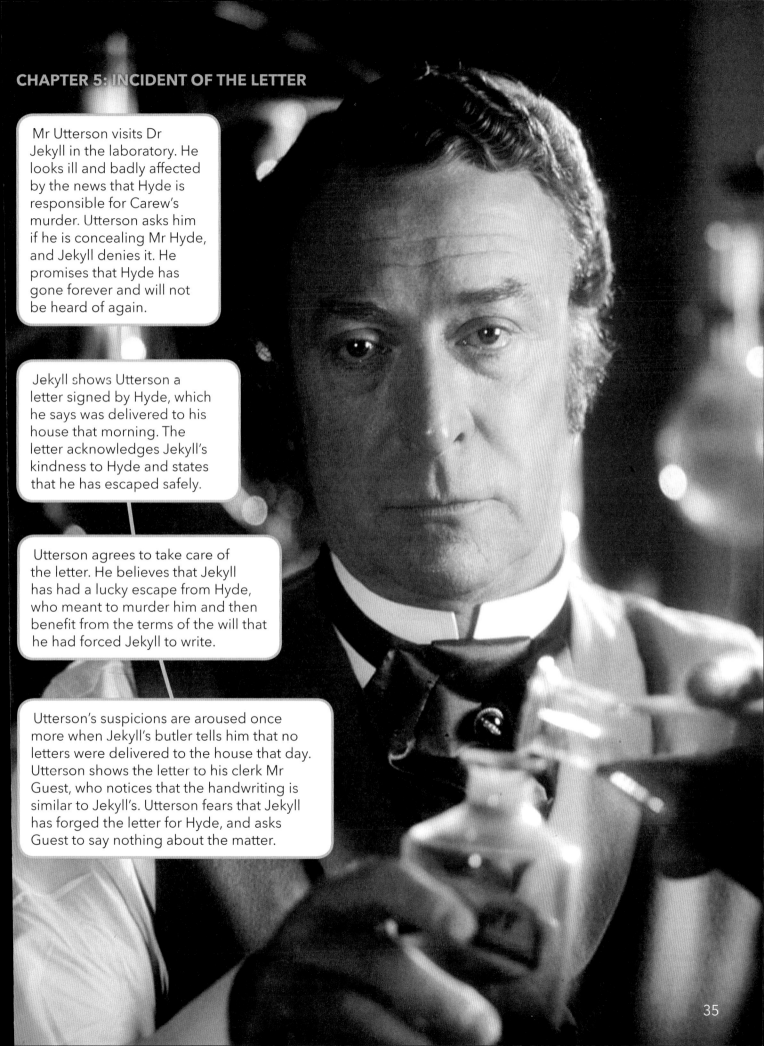

Mr Utterson visits Dr Jekyll in the laboratory. He looks ill and badly affected by the news that Hyde is responsible for Carew's murder. Utterson asks him if he is concealing Mr Hyde, and Jekyll denies it. He promises that Hyde has gone forever and will not be heard of again.

Jekyll shows Utterson a letter signed by Hyde, which he says was delivered to his house that morning. The letter acknowledges Jekyll's kindness to Hyde and states that he has escaped safely.

Utterson agrees to take care of the letter. He believes that Jekyll has had a lucky escape from Hyde, who meant to murder him and then benefit from the terms of the will that he had forced Jekyll to write.

Utterson's suspicions are aroused once more when Jekyll's butler tells him that no letters were delivered to the house that day. Utterson shows the letter to his clerk Mr Guest, who notices that the handwriting is similar to Jekyll's. Utterson fears that Jekyll has forged the letter for Hyde, and asks Guest to say nothing about the matter.

2 Write a paragraph comparing the description of the back of Jekyll's home in Chapter 5 with the following description of the front of the house from Chapter 2:

> … a large, low-roofed, comfortable hall, paved with flags, warmed (after the fashion of a country house) by a bright, open fire, and furnished with costly cabinets of oak.

Chapter 2

3 Jekyll's building can be seen as a **symbol** for an important **theme** in the novel – duality. In pairs, talk about the ideas you think are conveyed by the descriptions of two sides of the same building.

PUTTING DETAILS TO USE

Dr Jekyll's changing character

1 Stevenson shows a change in the **character** of Dr Jekyll at this point in the story. Copy and complete the following table to show how he is described in Chapter 3 and in Chapter 5.

Description from Chapter 3	Contrasting quotation from Chapter 5
'a large well-made man'	
'sincere and warm affection'	
'carried it off gaily'	
'every mark of capacity and kindness'	

2 Read aloud Jekyll's words from the first two pages of Chapter 5. How has Stevenson made him seem '**feverish**'? You may find it useful to look for examples of:

a repetition
b short sentences
c hesitation
d emphasis.

The letter as a plot device

1 Put the following statements about the letter in the order they are revealed in the chapter.

a Jekyll says he burned the envelope.
b The letter is written in an '**odd, upright hand**'.
c The letter reassures Mr Utterson about the relationship between Jekyll and Hyde.
d Jekyll says the letter was handed in at the house, not posted.
e Utterson shows the letter to his chief clerk, who says the handwriting could be Jekyll's.
f Jekyll tells Utterson he has received a letter from Hyde and wonders whether to show it to the police.
g Poole tells Utterson that no letters arrived at the house that day.

2 How do you think the incident of the letter adds to the mystery and develops the plot?

 Watch Utterson and Guest examine the handwriting in the letter on Cambridge Elevate.

Secrets and silence

We know from what the characters say – or don't say – that several of them are keeping secrets.

1 Find the following quotations in Chapter 5 and identify which character they are referring to.

a **locked the note into his safe**
b **'I wouldn't speak of this note, you know'**
c **There was no man from whom he kept fewer secrets**
d **he shut his mouth tight and nodded**
e **'You do not know him as I do'**
f **'I cannot share with anyone'.**

2 Write a paragraph exploring how Stevenson has made the characters seem secretive. Use short quotations to support your points.

'The fogs of London'

Once again, the London fog provides a backdrop to events in this chapter.

 Copy the following table and draw lines to match the quotations with the appropriate analysis and comment.

Quotation	Analysis and comment
'even in the house the fog began to lie thickly'	A description that appeals to the reader's sense of hearing to show the effect of fog.
'foggy cupola'	A bird-like metaphor to show fog as a living thing.
'The fog still slept on the wing above the drowned city'	The fog masks even the features that should let in the light.
'the muffle and smother of these fallen clouds'	A description that shows the fog penetrating everywhere.

✔ **Learning checkpoint**

Write a short essay explaining how Stevenson uses fog to convey ideas in the novel. Use what you learnt in Unit 4 and your notes from 'The fogs of London' activity here. Here are some suggestions for points to include in your answer:

- examples of images of fog in the novel
- significance of fog in 19th-century London
- link between fog and mystery and confusion
- link between fog and nightmares or concealment.

Try to include key words such as 'symbol' and 'metaphor' in your writing.

 Key terms

symbol: an object used to represent something else.

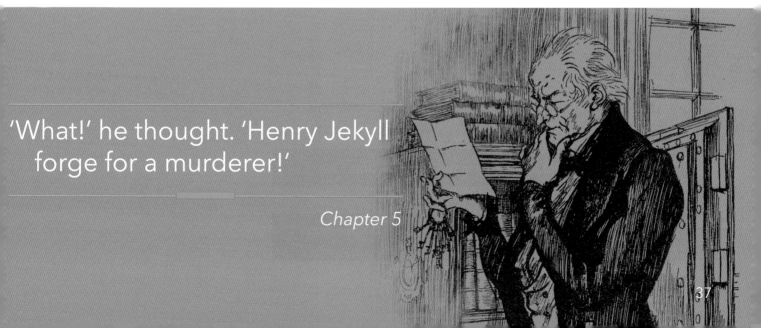

'What!' he thought. 'Henry Jekyll forge for a murderer!'

Chapter 5

The use of metaphors to present emotions and ideas

Metaphors express ideas and emotions in interesting ways to convey subtle meanings.

1 Copy and complete the following table to explain some of the metaphors in Chapter 5. In the third column, add information about the associations the metaphors may have and the ideas they convey. The first one has been done as an example.

Metaphor	Literal meaning	Possible associations and ideas
'blood ran cold in his veins'	The temperature of his blood dropped.	The idea of shivering with fear and dread.
'I have had a lesson'		
'sucked down in the eddy of the scandal'		
'the procession of the town's life was still rolling in through the great arteries'		
'the glow of hot autumn afternoons on hillside vineyards, was ready to be set free'		

Developing tension

Stevenson uses Utterson's investigations, discoveries and false conclusions to build tension and keep his readers interested as the story develops.

1 Create a graph to plot the changing tension in Chapter 5. Rank each of the following events 0 to 10, then plot them on a copy of the graph shown here. Join the points to see how the tension rises and falls.

a Utterson fears Jekyll is hiding Hyde.
b Hyde's letter suggests that he has escaped.
c Utterson believes Jekyll has had a lucky escape.
d Poole says no letter arrived.
e Utterson worries that scandal will damage Jekyll's reputation.
f Utterson relaxes by the fire.
g The handwriting on the letter is Jekyll's.
h Utterson fears that Jekyll forged the letter for a murderer.

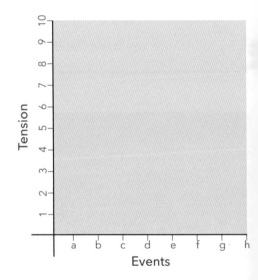

 Find out more about language in the novel in Unit 15.

 Watch two actors discussing how to maintain the tension for a modern audience on Cambridge Elevate.

GETTING IT INTO WRITING

Writing about minor characters

You have looked at how Stevenson presents some of the main characters in the novel. Now consider some of the minor characters.

 1 Select two minor characters from the story so far. You could choose from:

- the maidservant who witnessed the murder
- Hyde's housekeeper
- Mr Enfield
- Inspector Newcomen.

Write three or four paragraphs describing the role of your two characters. Explain:

a who they are
b how Stevenson presents them
c what you think they contribute to the development of the plot
d what you think they contribute to our understanding of events and ideas.

Use the sample answer, about the minor character Mr Guest, as a guide for your own writing.

✓ Complete this assignment on Cambridge Elevate.

GETTING FURTHER

Plotting the tension

1 Draw a tension graph to plot the details of Utterson's mood and level of concern about the mystery at the start and end of the first five chapters of the novel.

2 What do you think your graph reveals about Stevenson's approach to structuring the story? Why do you think this?

Sample answer:

Mr Guest is Utterson's trusted clerk, 'a man of counsel', and the person he turns to for advice. As a lawyer, Utterson is very discreet, but 'there was no man from whom he kept fewer secrets than Mr Guest'. Even so, Utterson has to think carefully before showing him such an important letter from Mr Hyde. Stevenson shows Utterson's thought process through **rhetorical questions** as he considers what to do.

Mr Guest is important to the plot because he is 'a great student and critic of handwriting'. He is intrigued to see a letter written by the murderer, and studies it 'with passion'. Coincidentally, a note arrives from Dr Jekyll inviting Utterson to dinner. When Guest compares Jekyll's handwriting with Hyde's letter, he finds a similarity.

This kind of scientific approach to solving crimes would have been familiar to the readers of detective fiction that became popular during the 19th century. Utterson is shocked and worried by the suggestion that Jekyll forged the note for Hyde. He asks Guest not to say any more about it and, when Guest agrees, he becomes another character keeping up respectable appearances by hiding secrets.

clear opening with a good quotation to show understanding of character
comments on the effect of language
reference to the text used with embedded quotation
points out links between events
comments on historical context
makes links between character and ideas or themes

 Key terms

rhetorical question: a question intended to make a point rather than requiring an answer.

6

Shocks and changes

How does Stevenson develop his characters?

GETTING STARTED – THE STORY AND YOU

Expressions using body parts

There are many **idiomatic expressions** in the English language that refer to parts of the body. We use these as ways of expressing feelings and emotions that we all share.

1 Work in small groups. Take it in turns to choose one of the following idiomatic expressions. Act out its literal and then its metaphorical meaning while the others in the group try to guess which expression you have chosen.

a crying your eyes out
b putting your foot in it
c letting your hair down
d doing your head in
e being thick-skinned.

These phrases reflect the idea that feelings can cause physical reactions. In Stevenson's day, people believed that someone's mental or emotional state could affect their physical condition and cause illness.

2 Work in pairs. Discuss the emotions you think are associated with the physical details in these idiomatic expressions.

a to be sick to death of something
b to find something heart-warming
c to get cold feet
d to be out of your mind
e to get something off your chest
f to make your skin crawl.

 Watch a summary of 'Remarkable incident of Doctor Lanyon' on Cambridge Elevate.

 Key terms

idiomatic expression: a creative phrase that people who speak the same language will understand (e.g. to 'make a clean breast of something' means to confess what you have done).

The police are unable to find Mr Hyde. More stories emerge about his cruelty and odd behaviour, but it is as if he never existed.

Mr Utterson begins to feel more relaxed. Dr Jekyll starts a new life, socialising with friends, supporting charities and practising religion.

This behaviour stops abruptly. Jekyll suddenly withdraws from society and refuses to see anyone. Utterson repeatedly tries to visit him but is turned away each time.

Utterson visits his friend Dr Lanyon and is shocked to find him very ill – on the brink of death. Lanyon explains that he has had a terrible shock, from which he can never recover.

All ties between Lanyon and Jekyll have been broken, and both men say that their friendship is finished. Two weeks later, Lanyon dies.

Utterson receives a package from Lanyon and finds inside a sealed envelope with instructions that it must be opened only on the death or disappearance of Dr Jekyll. These words remind Utterson of Jekyll's will. He is concerned and curious, but he behaves honourably, locking the letter in his safe.

Utterson tries again to visit Jekyll but the butler tells him that Jekyll will see no one and spends most of his time in the 'cabinet' – his room above the laboratory.

GETTING CLOSER – FOCUS ON DETAILS

The change in Dr Lanyon

Stevenson uses the metaphor **'his death warrant written legibly upon his face'** to describe the change in Lanyon's appearance. Look at the description of Dr Lanyon in the 'Getting further' section of Unit 2. Then look at this description of him from Chapter 6:

The rosy man had grown pale; his flesh had fallen away; he was visibly balder and older; and yet it was not so much these tokens of a swift physical decay that arrested the lawyer's notice, as a look in the eye and quality of manner that seemed to testify to some deep-seated terror of the mind.

Chapter 6

1 Work in pairs. Identify the contrasts that Stevenson makes in these descriptions.

2 Discuss Stevenson's representation of Lanyon's physical condition. What experiences do you think have made it change so much between Chapter 2 and Chapter 6?

PUTTING DETAILS TO USE

The change in Dr Jekyll

1 Dr Jekyll could be considered a changeable **character** in his behaviour and attitudes. Do you agree with this interpretation? Why, or why not?

2 For each of the following quotations, identify the chapter and the speaker or the character it is referring to. Then make a note of whether you think the impression it gives is good or bad and explain the reasons for your interpretation.

   a   'the very pink of the proprieties, celebrated too [...] one of your fellows who do what they call good'
   b   'Henry Jekyll became too fanciful for me. He began to go wrong, wrong in mind'
   c   'He was wild when he was young'
   d   a large, well-made, smooth-faced man of fifty, with something of a slyish cast perhaps, but every mark of capacity and kindness
   e   looking deadly sick. He did not rise to meet his visitor, but held out a cold hand and bade him welcome in a changed voice.

3 At the start of Chapter 6, with Hyde gone, **'a new life began for Dr Jekyll'**. This lasts for more than two months and brings him feelings of peace. However, by the end of the chapter, Jekyll has once more returned to a life of **'extreme seclusion'**.

Look at the following possible causes for the change in Jekyll's behaviour. Which reasons do you think are most likely? Rate each reason 1 to 5, where 1 is a very likely cause and 5 is very unlikely. Find evidence in the text to support your choices.

a   Jekyll is troubled by the fear that some guilty secret from his past will be revealed and ruin his reputation.

b   He has come to hate and despise his former friends and no longer wants to associate with them.

c   He is being kept inside his house against his will.

d   Mr Hyde is influencing him.

e   He feels that he has sinned and is being justly punished for it.

f   He is on the brink of madness.

Learning checkpoint

Write a paragraph to summarise your thoughts on the most likely cause or causes of Jekyll's strange behaviour. Give details from the text to justify your response.

How will I know I've done this well?

✔ **The best answers** will give a well-structured argument about Jekyll's motives based on confident interpretation of precise details from the text. They will explore ideas and contextual factors linked to his behaviour, analysing how Stevenson's language shapes their understanding.

✔ **Good answers** will show a developed response to Jekyll which uses appropriate references to the text and comments on the writer's methods. They might explain some ideas and contextual factors.

✔ **Weaker answers** will make simple, supported comments on Jekyll's behaviour. They may identify examples of the writer's methods and comment on the explicit ideas they convey.

Ideas about sin and disgrace

Utterson believes that Jekyll is hiding some 'disgrace'. Victorian readers would have recognised that this hints at sexual misbehaviour. Do you think Stevenson is using the character of Utterson to deliberately mislead his readers?

1   Look at the following information. What do these details suggest to you about the secret lives of the characters? Remember – Stevenson deliberately leaves things open to a range of interpretations.

a   Respectable men such as Mr Enfield and Sir Danvers Carew are found in odd places in London at the dead of night.

b   Lanyon, who is a doctor, knows a dreadful secret about Jekyll.

c   Jekyll writes to Utterson that he has brought on himself a punishment and danger that he cannot name. He describes himself as '**The chief of sinners**'.

d   Jekyll punishes himself by cutting himself off from the outside world.

2   Look at the following possible reasons for Jekyll's behaviour. In pairs, discuss any evidence you can find for each reason.

a   financial problems and blackmail

b   forgery and hiding a murderer

c   previous sexual behaviour

d   madness.

Contexts

Attitudes towards sexual behaviour in the 19th century were different from modern attitudes. 'Respectable' people did not discuss sexuality. and homosexual activity was against the law. Many people kept their behaviour a secret.

The sexually transmitted disease syphilis was a widespread problem for which there was no cure at the time. Some religious people and medical professionals believed that it was a punishment for casual sex or immoral behaviour.

Narrative structure

Stevenson uses several different techniques to keep the story interesting. One of these is to include written documents, such as letters and notes.

1 Look back through the novel and list all the written documents that have been mentioned so far. Add a note explaining why you think each one is important.

The action of the story takes place over a long period of time. This helps to build suspense, as well as making the story seem more realistic.

2 Work in groups of six. Each person takes a chapter and skim reads it to identify references to the following. Pay particular attention to the opening paragraphs in each chapter.

- a time of day
- b days of the week
- c months
- d seasons
- e time passing.

3 Share your findings with the rest of the group. Draw a timeline of events. Leave space after Chapter 6 so you can add more details as you read on.

- a How much time passes between Chapter 1 and Chapter 6?
- b In which season of the year does the action take place?

 Find out more about plot and structure in the novel in Unit 11.

GETTING IT INTO WRITING

Choosing appropriate vocabulary

When writing about *The Strange Case of Dr Jekyll and Mr Hyde*, choosing the right vocabulary is an important way of showing how well you have understood the novel.

1 The words in the word bank are related to the same idea, but they all have slightly different meanings. Look these words up in a dictionary to make sure you understand what they mean.

puzzling	mysterious	obscure
unclear	enigmatic	ambiguous
vague	evasive	intriguing

2 Write a paragraph on each of the following details from the text, explaining how you think they add suspense to the novel. Use the words from the word bank.

 a   Dr Lanyon's comments about his relationship with Jekyll.
 b   The changes in Jekyll's behaviour.
 c   The contents of Jekyll's letter to Utterson.
 d   The details of the package that Mr Utterson opens from Dr Lanyon after his death.

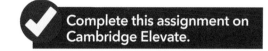

Complete this assignment on Cambridge Elevate.

GETTING FURTHER

Keeping secrets

The **theme** of secrets and concealment is important in all mystery stories. Stevenson uses **imagery** of doors, locks and safes to suggest that the characters are hiding the truth.

1 List all the examples you can find where doors, locks and safes are mentioned in Chapters 1–5.

2 Re-read Chapter 6. Identify references to the following:

 a   openness and confinement
 b   closed or locked doors
 c   sealed documents
 d   safe places.

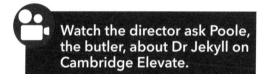

Watch the director ask Poole, the butler, about Dr Jekyll on Cambridge Elevate.

3 Summarise your thoughts in a paragraph starting with this sentence:

Stevenson uses the symbolism of locked doors and sealed documents to suggest …

'If I am the chief of sinners, I am the chief of sufferers also.'

Jekyll: Chapter 6

7

The calm before the storm

How does Stevenson use symbolism and contrast?

Your progress in this unit:
- understand the significance of events in this short chapter
- understand how Jekyll's behaviour is presented
- explore Stevenson's use of symbolism and contrast.

GETTING STARTED – THE STORY AND YOU

Writers and film directors often create drama by introducing a sudden surprise to a peaceful or happy scene.

1 Write down some examples of this type of contrast that you have read or seen in books and films. Share your examples with a partner and discuss what makes them effective.

Think about the situation by the end of Chapter 6 in *The Strange Case of Dr Jekyll and Mr Hyde*. After all the strange events and mystery, Hyde has disappeared, Lanyon is dead and Utterson has stopped visiting Jekyll. Is the story of Jekyll and Hyde over?

2 Work with a partner to predict what might happen next.

GETTING CLOSER – FOCUS ON DETAILS

Read the summary. Then read Chapter 7.

In search of forgiveness

Mr Utterson's last words in Chapter 7 are: **'God forgive us, God forgive us.'**

1 What do you think Utterson means by these words? Who needs forgiveness? For what? Why do you think this?

2 What is the effect of the repetition here?

Watch a performance of 'Incident at the window' on Cambridge Elevate.

PUTTING DETAILS TO USE

The significance of Sundays

Until about 50 years ago in England, Sunday was a holy day for Christians, when businesses were closed and people enjoyed a day of rest. Stevenson points out how quiet the street is compared with the bustle of weekdays.

1 Work in pairs.

a Discuss the meaning of a holy day or day of rest.

b Talk about what you think are the effects of setting both visits to the street on Sundays.

On a Sunday afternoon, Utterson and Enfield walk down the same street as before. They discuss the building that Enfield now knows is the rear entrance to Jekyll's house.

Utterson feels that Jekyll might need a friend, so they look for him at his windows. Jekyll is sitting at one window sadly looking out like a prisoner. He greets them in a friendly way, but says he dare not join them in their walk.

Utterson offers to stay and talk to him, but suddenly Jekyll's expression changes to one of terror and despair. He slams the window shut and disappears inside.

Utterson and Enfield are shocked into silence as they continue their walk.

Contrasts in speech and behaviour

1 Look at the **dialogue** between Utterson and Jekyll in Chapter 7, and at the way the two men act.

   a What contrasts can you find in their speech and behaviour?

   b What do you think these differences suggest about the two men?

   c What impression does the dialogue convey of the men's different moods and feelings?

2 Find words and phrases in the text that describe how Jekyll's expression changes at the end of the chapter. What do you think causes this sudden change?

Learning checkpoint

Think about how Stevenson presents the relationships between Utterson, Enfield and Jekyll in Chapter 7. With a partner or in a group, discuss how you think Stevenson uses their relationships to explore ideas about mystery and concealment.

Try to find evidence in the novel for each point that you make. Remember to consider Stevenson's language and the effects it has on you as the reader.

The power of unstated horror

Stevenson does not explain what happens in Jekyll's room at the end of this chapter. Instead, he shows the dramatic effect that it has on Jekyll and consequently on the two men outside the window.

Read the following extracts, and the annotations that describe Stevenson's use of language.

> … the smile was struck out of his face and succeeded by an expression of such abject terror …

Chapter 7

The strong contrast between the happiness of a '**smile**' and the expression of '**abject terror**' shows how Jekyll experiences extreme emotions.

> … froze the very blood of the two gentlemen below.

Chapter 7

The **metaphor** of frozen blood exaggerates the idea of something chilling and shows Utterson's and Enfield's feelings of terror.

Do you agree with the interpretations in the annotations? Before you do Activity 1, think about any points you could add or changes you would make to the analyses.

1 Now analyse the following quotations. Use the sentence starters provided to help you explain the effects.

   a '**They saw it but for a glimpse**'
This reference to time and the shortness of a 'glimpse' creates mystery because …

   b '**They were both pale; and there was an answering horror in their eyes.**'
Stevenson describes the men's physical response to show their feelings of …

 Watch actors performing a 'marking the moment' activity for this chapter on Cambridge Elevate.

GETTING IT INTO WRITING

Writing about the false sense of closure

At the start of Chapter 7, Utterson and Enfield express satisfaction that the unpleasant business with Hyde is over. However, it soon becomes clear that the mystery has not been solved.

1 Write two paragraphs explaining how Chapter 7 develops the plot and **characters**. Use the prompts in the spider diagram to help you.

 Complete this assignment on Cambridge Elevate.

It is ironic that Enfield says 'that story's at an end at least' when later …

At the end of Chapter 6, Utterson was no longer in contact with Jekyll, so this incident …

Developing plot

The effect of the strong contrast between the start and end of this chapter is …

GETTING FURTHER

The symbolism of windows

1 Work in pairs. Discuss how windows might be used as **symbols** to represent ideas. Think about window openings, the transparency of glass, the protection windows provide from the outside world.

2 Write a paragraph explaining how you think Stevenson uses the window in this chapter to present ideas about Jekyll. Think about:

a   the half-open window
b   Jekyll's feelings about coming out
c   the window 'instantly thrust down'.

He is deeply affected by …

Developing characters

Jekyll's mood appears to be …

Utterson is shown as …

the smile was struck out of his face and succeeded by an expression of such abject terror …

Chapter 7

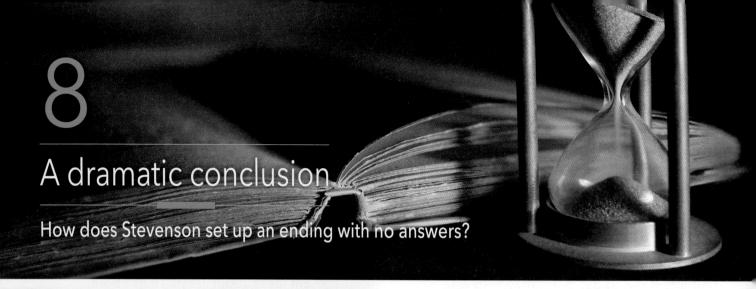

8

A dramatic conclusion

How does Stevenson set up an ending with no answers?

GETTING STARTED – THE STORY AND YOU

Servants and social class

Various minor **characters** from the lower classes appear in the novel. They include Poole (Dr Jekyll's butler), the maid who witnesses Carew's murder and Mr Hyde's housekeeper.

1 In pairs, discuss the relationship between servants and their employers. Consider the following questions:

a What might have been expected on each side?

b Why might writers use servants' **testimony** about other characters and events?

c Find out what the word 'deference' means and discuss its link with social class. Do you think ideas about deference have changed over time? If so, in what ways have they changed?

GETTING CLOSER – FOCUS ON DETAILS

Read the summary. Then read Chapter 8.

Considering Poole as a narrative device

During Poole's previous brief appearances in the novel, he is simply the butler calmly carrying out his duties. In Chapter 8, however, Stevenson describes Poole's emotions and behaviour. Here, he becomes an important witness to events that have occurred inside Jekyll's house.

1 Read the account of Poole's arrival at Utterson's house. Find at least two details from the text to support each of these statements about him:

a Poole's arrival shocks Utterson.

b Poole's appearance and manner make him seem ill.

c Poole is unwilling or unable to explain what is wrong.

d Poole is very frightened.

2 Utterson questions Poole, as he has questioned other characters. He can see that **'there is something seriously amiss'**, but Poole only says that he thinks there has been **'foul play'**.

a Do you think Poole's account seems vague or precise? Which words make you think this?

b Do you think there is anything he is not saying? If so, what might this be?

c How do his words help to increase tension and build suspense for the reader?

Poole calls on Utterson to appeal for help because he fears 'foul play'. They go to Jekyll's house, and Poole leads Utterson to the door of Jekyll's room.

When they knock, a voice tells them to go away. Poole says the voice is not Jekyll's and he believes that murder has been committed. He explains that Jekyll has not been seen for a week, although he has passed out orders for a particular drug. Poole has taken the orders to various chemists with no success. He has also heard footsteps pacing the floor and the sound of weeping.

Utterson and Poole suspect that Hyde has killed Jekyll and that it is his voice they hear. They break down the door.

Inside is the dead body of Hyde. Beside him is an empty poison bottle, suggesting that he killed himself. Jekyll is nowhere to be found, but Utterson and Poole cannot see how he could have left.

Searching the room they find chemicals, a large mirror and a religious book covered in blasphemies (words against God) in Jekyll's handwriting. On the desk is a package addressed to Utterson containing three documents: Jekyll's revised will, a note telling Utterson to read Lanyon's narrative and Jekyll's sealed confession.

PUTTING DETAILS TO USE

Increasing tension through description

Poole's mood seems to affect Utterson. He feels **'a crushing anticipation of calamity'** as they travel to Jekyll's house. Even the weather appears troubled, and Stevenson uses **pathetic fallacy** to describe a stormy scene filled with foreboding.

It was a wild, cold, seasonable night of March, with a pale moon, lying on her back as though the wind had tilted her, and a flying wrack of the most diaphanous and lawny texture. […] The square, when they got there, was all full of wind and dust, and the thin trees in the garden were lashing themselves along the railing.

Chapter 8

---

1 Use the internet to find images that reflect the description in this passage. Put these together to create a 'mood board'.

2 Copy out the passage in the middle of the mood board, then around it write up to four headings that reflect the **themes** in the passage and your images. For example one heading could be 'Details about time'.

Under each heading, identify relevant words and phrases from the text, then explain the effects they create. Try to use the following words in your explanations: **adjectives**, **personification**, **sensual appeal**, **onomatopoeia**.

Exploring the gothic atmosphere

The effects discussed in this unit are common features of gothic literature. Look at this extract:

The scud had banked over the moon, and it was now quite dark. The wind, which only broke in puffs and draughts into that deep well of building, tossed the light of the candle to and fro about their steps, until they came into the shelter of the theatre.

Chapter 8

 How have the natural conditions changed since the two men set off from Utterson's house? Discuss this in pairs.

2 In your pairs, talk about how you think this description appeals to the reader's senses.

ℹ Contexts

Gothic novels, which became popular in the late 18th century, explored ideas about death and passionate feelings that were often linked to the supernatural. Their **settings** were wild, dark and eerie, and they dealt with terrifying events. Gothic elements continue to be popular in literature and films – Mary Shelley's novel *Frankenstein* still grips readers 200 years after its first publication, for example. An example of a modern gothic horror is Susan Hill's novel *The Woman in Black* (1983), which has been adapted for the stage and film.

 Find out more about context and setting in the novel in Unit 12.

'Jangled nerves'

The disordered natural world that Stevenson presents is reflected inside the house – Jekyll's servants huddle together fearfully in a way that Utterson calls '**very irregular, very unseemly**'.

1 Read the section of Chapter 8 beginning '**Thereupon the servant knocked in a very guarded manner**' to '**now wept loudly**'. List all the words and phrases that suggest the servants are afraid.

Exploring characterisation and social class

Poole and the servants defer to Utterson because he has higher social status. He quickly takes charge, putting himself at the centre of the action.

1 Find short quotations from the text that support each of the following points.

a Poole and the servants are relieved to see Utterson.
b They use respectful language.
c Utterson speaks with authority.
d Poole defers to him in planning their actions.

2 Create a table with two columns, headed 'Rational thought' and 'Defies reason'. Look at the following list of things that Utterson says and copy each one into the appropriate column in your table.

a 'a very strange tale'
b 'a wild tale'
c 'That won't hold water; it doesn't commend itself to reason.'
d 'I think I begin to see daylight'
e 'There is my explanation'
f 'it is plain and natural'
g 'all exorbitant alarms'.

Key terms

pathetic fallacy: the idea that the natural world is sympathetic to people's experiences and feelings – for example using fog to suggest that it is difficult to see matters clearly.

personification: a type of metaphor that gives human qualities to inanimate objects.

sensual appeal: describing writing that appeals to a reader's senses, such as sight and hearing.

onomatopoeia: words that sound like the sounds they describe.

It was a wild, cold, seasonable night of March, with a pale moon, lying on her back as though the wind had tilted her

Chapter 8

Poole's role as the loyal servant

Poole is a witness to the appearance, habits and behaviour of both Dr Jekyll and Mr Hyde. His testimony might be considered reliable because he has worked for Jekyll for many years and has been in the house to see Hyde's comings and goings.

At the beginning of Chapter 8, Poole seems evasive: '**[he] had not once looked the lawyer in the face**'. This may be because he feels he is being disloyal to his master or because he is afraid of what is happening. Later, when Utterson says that they must be frank with each other and '**make a clean breast**' of their suspicions, Poole gives his opinion of Mr Hyde and says he was the '**masked figure**' in the laboratory.

Look at the following extract and annotations that show an analysis of how Stevenson presents Hyde in Poole's description:

'... there was something queer about that gentleman – something that gave a man a turn [...] you felt it in your marrow kind of cold and thin.

[...]

'Well, when that masked thing like a monkey jumped from among the chemicals and whipped into the cabinet, it went down my spine like ice.'

> **Metaphors** express physical reactions and create an impression of horror around Hyde.

> A **simile** compares Hyde to an animal, making him sound primitive and dangerous.

Poole: Chapter 8

1 Are there any other points you could make to add to the analysis of this extract? Discuss them with a partner.

2 In your pairs, talk about how Poole's description in the extract supports the following ideas about Mr Hyde:

  a People are disturbed by his appearance.
  b He is like an animal.
  c He moves quickly.

In contrast, Poole shows his respect for Jekyll:

'My master [...] is a tall, fine build of a man [...] do you think I do not know my master after twenty years? do you think I do not know where his head comes to in the cabinet door, where I saw him every morning of my life?'

Poole: Chapter 8

3 Are there any details in this extract which show that Poole can be relied upon as a witness about Jekyll? If so, what are they?

Religious references

The religious language that Stevenson gives the characters in this chapter reflects the **context** of England in the 19th century. Afraid of what is happening behind the closed doors in Jekyll's house, the characters call on God for courage and help.

1 Work in pairs. Look through the chapter and find out who speaks the following words. For each one, explain what you think leads the character to put their hope in God:

   a   'God grant there be nothing wrong.'
   b   'God grant that he be not deceived!'
   c   'God grant I have no cause for it!'

2 Find the following words and phrases in Chapter 8 and identify the characters that say them:

   a   'Bless me!'
   b   'Amen'
   c   'For God's sake …'
   d   'Bless God!'
   e   '… a thing that cries to Heaven'.

3 How do you think these references to God and religion might add to ideas about good and evil in the novel? Write a short paragraph explaining your ideas.

Learning checkpoint

Check that you have understood Poole's testimony by writing brief notes on the evidence he gives about:

✔ the voice
✔ the notes to the chemist
✔ the handwriting on the notes
✔ the person he saw in the laboratory
✔ the length of time since he saw Jekyll.

Key terms

context: the historical circumstances of a piece of writing, which affect what an author wrote and the way they wrote it.

Watch an adaptation of Utterson visiting Jekyll on Cambridge Elevate.

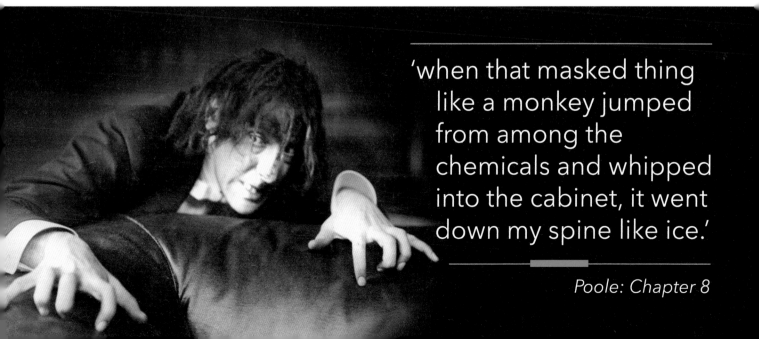

'when that masked thing like a monkey jumped from among the chemicals and whipped into the cabinet, it went down my spine like ice.'

Poole: Chapter 8

Exploring dramatic action

Stevenson was skilled at creating puzzles and building clues. These create mystery in his stories and make the action exciting and dramatic.

1 Work in groups of four. Read the section in which Utterson and Poole break down the door, from '**But now the ten minutes …**' to '**… most commonplace that night in London**'.

Imagine you have been asked to direct a film version of the scene. Write notes on how you would show the action. Remember to think about the effect you want to have on your audience. Use the following prompts to start you off.

Include:

1 Introduce the production team to the scene and explain the effects you want to achieve.

2 Details of the set: how to show both outside and inside the door and what the door looks like.

3 Directions for the actors: Poole, Utterson, the speaker inside the room.

4 List of props: how they contribute to the impression you want to create.

5 Camera angles and close-ups: what the audience will see.

6 Sound effects: what the audience will hear.

Identifying and explaining the effects of horror

The events in this chapter seem dangerous and terrifying. Once again, Stevenson shows how fear and other emotions have a physical effect on the characters.

1 Which events in this chapter do you think have the following effects on Poole and Utterson? For each one, identify the emotion that the character is experiencing.

a   **Mr Utterson's nerves […] gave a jerk that nearly threw him from his balance.**

b   **'The hair stood upon my head like quills'**

c   The butler turned '**to a sort of mottled pallor**'

d   **'Something that gave a man a turn […] felt in your marrow kind of cold and thin'**

e   **a sudden chill of horror**

f   **with bated breath.**

2 Read Poole's description of what he hears in the room behind the closed door, and the effect it has on him.

    a How does he explain the weeping?

    b Why do you think the person in the room weeps?

Drawing conclusions

At the end of the chapter, Utterson admits to Poole, '**My head goes round**'. Even though the notes to the chemist were written in Jekyll's handwriting, Poole does not believe the person in the room is his master, because neither the voice he hears nor the figure he sees belong to Jekyll.

1 What conclusion has Poole reached about what has happened?

2 Utterson's conclusion is based on Jekyll's eagerness to obtain the drug. What do you think he means when he says that Jekyll must have been '**seized with one of those maladies that both torture and deform the sufferer**'?

Although the notes to the chemist and the letter to Utterson prove that Jekyll was alive earlier the same day, he has now completely disappeared. Yet Utterson and Poole cannot see how Jekyll could have left the room.

3 Hyde lies dead on the floor in clothes that are '**far too large for him**'.

    a How does this fit with what Stevenson has shown about Hyde earlier in the novel?

    b Identify any animal **imagery** and references to Hyde's disturbing appearance that you can find in Poole's account.

GETTING IT INTO WRITING

Writing about Utterson

This is the last time that Utterson appears in the novel – he is not the person who reveals the answer to the mystery.

1 Write two or three paragraphs in response to the following questions:

    a How does Stevenson present Utterson in this chapter? Do you think he plays a key role? Why, or why not?

    b How important do you think Utterson's role is in the novel as a whole? Give reasons for your answer.

 Complete this assignment on Cambridge Elevate.

 Watch two actors discuss how Stevenson builds tension and drama in this chapter on Cambridge Elevate.

GETTING FURTHER

Themes and ideas

1 Using examples from Chapter 8, add to the notes you made in previous units on the following themes and ideas:

    a documents

    b doors and locks

    c silence or reluctance to talk.

2 Write a paragraph to suggest how these ideas have been developed in preparation for the mystery to be revealed. Consider the following:

    a The documents will be read.

    b The door has been broken down.

    c Lanyon and Jekyll are about to 'speak' through their accounts for Utterson.

9

The big reveal

How does Stevenson explain the mystery?

Your progress in this unit:
- understand the characters and events
- examine how Chapter 9 fits into the structure of the novel
- explore Stevenson's language and style at this point in the story
- consider how ideas about science and morality are presented.

GETTING STARTED – THE STORY AND YOU

The problems with science

Read the following newspaper headlines about scientific and medical procedures.

Frankenstein-style human head transplant 'could happen in two years'

Italian surgeon claims procedure to graft a living person's head on to a donor body will soon be ready

Three-parent babies: Britain becomes first country to allow technique after House of Lords approves new regulations

1 How much do the headlines tell you about the science behind the stories?

2 How do the headlines suggest that science is scary or dangerous?

GETTING CLOSER – FOCUS ON DETAILS

Read the summary. Then read Chapter 9.

The ingredients of a great conclusion

A key feature of detective fiction is the moment of revelation – when the expert draws together all the clues and explains the events in the story.

1 Work in small groups. List any books, TV programmes and films that use the dramatic device of the moment of revelation.

In *The Strange Case of Dr Jekyll and Mr Hyde*, Mr Utterson has investigated and encountered many clues. However, Stevenson does not use him to reveal the mystery. Instead, after the dramatic events described in Chapter 8, Stevenson directs the reader's attention to Dr Lanyon's narrative and the other document '**in which the mystery was now to be explained**'.

2 Remind yourself of the things that still need to be explained about each of the following at this point in the story. Write a couple of notes or questions for each one.

- a Dr Jekyll
- b Mr Hyde
- c The urgent orders for drugs
- d The mirror in Jekyll's room.

 Watch an adaptation of Lanyon watching Jekyll's transformation on Cambridge Elevate.

This is a **first-person narrative** describing events that take place in January. Lanyon reports that he unexpectedly received a letter from Dr Jekyll, which appealed for his help on a matter of life and death.

The letter asked Lanyon to meet Poole at Jekyll's house. A locksmith would break into Jekyll's room, and Jekyll asked Lanyon to enter, bring out a drawer containing chemicals, and take it back to his own house. At midnight he should expect a visit from a man on Jekyll's behalf; he should give the contents of the drawer to him.

Lanyon follows the instructions. The man who appears at midnight is small with a disturbing appearance. He does not give his name and Lanyon has never seen him before. The visitor eagerly takes the drawer's contents and mixes the chemicals into a strange compound.

Holding it up, he gives Lanyon the choice to stay and see its effects or to remain in ignorance. Lanyon stays and is sworn to secrecy as a doctor. The man drinks the mixture and transforms into Jekyll. Lanyon is overcome by the horror of what he witnesses and what Jekyll has told him.

🔑 Key terms

first-person narrative: an account of events using the pronouns 'I', 'me' and 'we'.

PUTTING DETAILS TO USE

Understanding the events explained in Lanyon's narrative

Lanyon's **testimony** eventually provides an explanation of the mystery, but Stevenson maintains suspense all the way through it.

 Examine how Stevenson builds suspense by identifying short quotations to illustrate the following details. The first one has been done as an example.

a   Lanyon is surprised to receive a registered letter from Jekyll.
'… a good deal surprised by this; for we were by no means in the habit of correspondence.'

b   The letter makes Jekyll seem desperate for Lanyon's help.

c   Lanyon believes that Jekyll must have gone mad.

d   Poole has also received a letter of instruction from Jekyll.

e   Lanyon is puzzled by the contents of the drawer that he collects from Jekyll's room.

f   Lanyon cannot understand why Jekyll's **'messenger'** could not have collected the drawer directly from Jekyll's house.

g   Lanyon anticipates trouble and arms himself with a revolver for self-defence.

h   The man who arrives at midnight behaves suspiciously.

i   Lanyon does not know him.

j   The visitor's appearance is strange.

k   He mixes the chemicals with dramatic results.

How does Stevenson create impact at the moment of revelation?

Lanyon shows both confusion and concern from the moment he receives Jekyll's letter to the point when his visitor mixes the chemicals. Stevenson heightens the drama by making the stranger pause, put down the chemicals and ask Lanyon to choose whether or not to stay to see what happens.

 Read the visitor's words aloud:

> 'Will you be wise? will you be guided? will you suffer me to take this glass in my hand and to go forth from your house without further parley? or has the greed of curiosity too much command of you? Think before you answer, for it shall be done as you decide.'

Hyde: Chapter 9

a   What do you notice about the sentences the visitor uses? Discuss this in pairs.

b   How do the sentences create suspense?

c   What do you think the visitor means by **'the greed of curiosity'**?

As a Christian, Lanyon would have recognised the **allusion** to Satan in this speech. Christians believe that Satan has great power to persuade humans to turn away from God towards the path of evil.

 Identify where the following persuasive devices occur in the visitor's speech.

a   **rhetorical questions**

b   **direct address to the listener**

c   **metaphor**

d   **appeal to emotions.**

🔑 Key terms

allusion: a reference to something that the listener or reader will recognise.

3 In pairs, read aloud the moment when the visitor drinks the chemical (from '**Behold! He put the glass to his lips**' to '**there stood Henry Jekyll!**') Then make notes on how the language of the passage creates a dramatic conclusion to the mystery. You could structure your notes in a table like this:

Quotation	Language feature	Interpretation of its effect
'he reeled, staggered, clutched at the table'	list of verbs	
'sprung to my feet and leaped back'	more active verbs	
'my mind submerged in terror'	metaphor of drowning	
'O God!' again and again	exclamation and repetition	

Remember – Lanyon does not know the identity of his visitor until the moment of revelation. Readers may identify Hyde from the clues in Lanyon's description, but it is not until the final sentence of this chapter that Lanyon confirms that '**The creature who crept into my house that night was […] known by the name of Hyde and hunted for in every corner of the land as the murderer of Carew.**'

4 Read the final paragraph of Chapter 9. How do you think Lanyon is affected by the knowledge that his friend Jekyll and the murderer Hyde are the same person? Find evidence in the text to support your answer.

 Find out more about plot and structure in the novel in Unit 11.

The creature who crept into my house that night was ... known by the name of Hyde

Lanyon: Chapter 9

The presentation of Lanyon through language

Up until Chapter 9, Stevenson writes from the point of view of a narrator who is outside the story and knows everything about the **characters** and events. He shapes the reader's understanding by the narrator's comments on the characters.

Here, however, Stevenson shifts the perspective to a first-person narrative. The whole of Chapter 9 is the account that Lanyon writes to Utterson before he dies. He includes in it the letter that Jekyll sent him. Stevenson gives Dr Lanyon a distinctive voice to make his character, emotions and opinions **authentic**.

1 Copy and complete the following table to examine how Stevenson presents Lanyon through his own voice. Some quotations have been provided to start you off, but you may be able to find more.

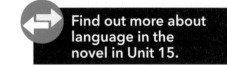

Find out more about language in the novel in Unit 15.

Quotations from Lanyon's speeches	Notes for analysis	How the voice shows Lanyon's character and matches what we know about him
'my colleague was insane' 'a case of cerebral disease'	medical expressions for diagnosis	
'simple crystalline salt … phosphorus … volatile ether'	precise names of chemicals	
'moral turpitude'		
'that man unveiled'		
'The deadliest terror sits by me'		

Using sentences to create tension

You have already seen how the structure of the novel leads to a dramatic revelation of the truth behind the mystery. Now examine how Stevenson constructs some sentences to create a similar effect.

Read aloud the following sentence from the end of the chapter. Notice that it carries the reader forward to the end, where the final two words contain the biggest shock.

Oh God!' I screamed [...] for there before my eyes – pale and shaken, and half-fainting, and groping before him with his hands, like a man restored from death – there stood Henry Jekyll!

Repetition for emphasis.

Dashes create the impression of natural speech as Lanyon breaks his sentence up by adding vivid detail.

Short descriptive phrases provide lots of information before the reader knows who is being described.

A **simile** makes the transformation seem other-worldly.

The writer delays the subject of the sentence until the end to heighten tension.

The exclamation mark reflects Lanyon's shock.

Learning checkpoint

Lanyon's account solves the mystery by showing the reader that Jekyll and Hyde are the same person. For the story to work well, it is important that Lanyon's testimony fits with what we already know.

Copy and complete the table to identify the links between details in Lanyon's narrative and those from earlier in the novel.

From Lanyon's narrative	Earlier details	Explanation of the link
Lanyon says these events happened on 9 January	early in Chapter 6	
Jekyll writes 'we … differed on scientific questions'	Chapter 3: Jekyll speaks to Utterson about Lanyon	
The door to Jekyll's room was very strong.	Chapter 8: Poole and Utterson break into the room	
The visitor avoids the police.	Chapter 5	
'I had never set eyes on him before'	Chapter 2	
The visitor receives the contents of the drawer with 'immense relief'.		
Lanyon says, 'I feel my days are numbered'.		
Lanyon uses Utterson's name in the final paragraph.		

Key terms

authentic: realistic and true to the character.

… pale and shaken, and half-fainting, and groping before him with his hands … stood Henry Jekyll

Lanyon: Chapter 9

Now look at the following extract:

'And now, you who have so long been bound to the most narrow and material views, you who have denied the virtue of transcendental medicine, you who have derided your superiors – behold!'

Hyde: Chapter 9

You could use the following as starting points for annotations:

- repetition of 'you'
- description of someone with status
- dash
- exclamation mark.

1 Copy out the extract, then expand the annotation suggestions and add more of your own to comment on the effects you think this sentence achieves.

The significance of time

Stevenson may have made a mistake when he dated Jekyll's letter to Lanyon 10th December. In Lanyon's account, it was written on 9th January – the same day that he received it. In the final chapter, Jekyll's statement also says that these events took place in January. Stevenson himself said that he wrote the novel at great speed, so perhaps he lost track of the dates.

1 In small groups, discuss how important you think it is to be accurate about details such as dates in a mystery novel.

The conflict between science and the imagination

In Chapter 2, Dr Lanyon explained that his friendship with Jekyll had broken down because he regarded Jekyll as having gone **'wrong in mind'** in his scientific beliefs. The end of their long-standing friendship reflects the two doctors' opposing attitudes towards science.

1 Look at the following spider diagrams, which show Lanyon and Jekyll's opinions about each other. For each quotation, write a note explaining what it shows about each man's views on science and the imagination.

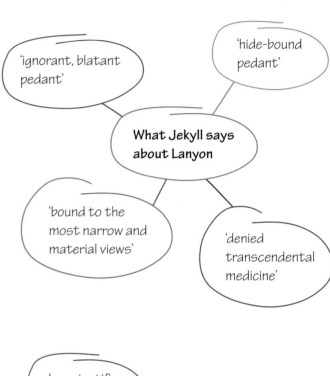

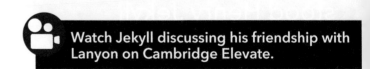

Watch Jekyll discussing his friendship with Lanyon on Cambridge Elevate.

GETTING IT INTO WRITING

Writing about linked passages

In the exam, you will be asked to write in detail about a passage from the text, then explore the points you make in relation to the novel as a whole.

1 Find two examples from the text so far where Jekyll either speaks or writes. Then write a short essay about how Stevenson uses language to present Jekyll in the extracts.

Use the following flow chart to help you plan and write your essay.

> Identify the impressions created in the first extract.

> How does the impression help the reader to understand Jekyll's state of mind? Support your interpretation by analysing words, phrases and sentences in the extract.

> Repeat the first two steps for the second extract.

> Include details about the similarities and differences between the two extracts.

 Complete this assignment on Cambridge Elevate.

GETTING FURTHER

The wonder of science

1 Read this extract describing the process of mixing the chemicals:

> 'the mixture […] began […] as the crystals melted, to brighten in colour, to effervesce audibly, and to throw off small fumes of vapour. Suddenly and at the same moment, the ebullition ceased and the compound changed to a dark purple, which faded again more slowly to a watery green.'

Lanyon: Chapter 9

- **a** Identify the colour changes that take place.
- **b** Find the words and phrases that appeal to the senses to give a vivid picture of what happened.
- **c** How do you think the description affects the way in which the reader regards this chemical mixture?

2 This description could be seen to represent the wonder of scientific discovery and chemical processes, showing the excitement of experimentation. Do you agree with this interpretation? Why, or why not? In groups, discuss how Stevenson presents science in this chapter and the moral issues he raises.

10

Dr Jekyll's own story

How does Stevenson explore the theme of good and evil?

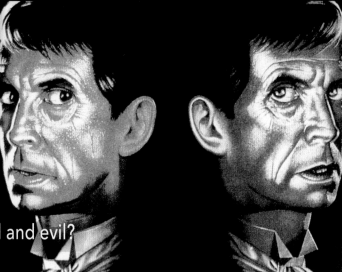

Your progress in this unit:
- understand Jekyll's account of his story
- examine the relationship between Dr Jekyll and Mr Hyde
- identify significant details to explore how Stevenson structures the novel
- explore ideas about the theme of good and evil.

GETTING STARTED – THE STORY AND YOU

Ending a story

1 Discuss examples of books and films that end in the following ways. How does each type of ending affect the reader or audience?

happiness ever after	a character getting what they deserve
sadness or death	a wedding
ellipsis, or a sense of being unfinished	an unexpected twist
revelation to explain a mystery	the hint of a sequel
	a moral message

2 Which types of ending might work for *The Strange Case of Dr Jekyll and Mr Hyde*? Why do you think this?

 Watch an adaptation of Jekyll's statement on Cambridge Elevate.

GETTING CLOSER – FOCUS ON DETAILS

Read the summary. Then read Chapter 10.

Understanding significant details

1 Read each of the following sections and make notes in answer to the questions. Find short quotations to support your comments.

a **'I was born … were they dissociated?'**
Find words and phrases meaning 'two' or 'doubles'. What ideas do they express about duality in human nature?

b **'I was so far in my reflection … I had lost in stature.'**
Look at language describing the first mixture and transformation. How does it show Jekyll's pleasure in evil?

c **'There was no mirror … toward the worse.'**
Identify important aspects of Hyde's appearance. What do they show about the balance between good and evil?

d **'Even at that time … the reach of fate.'**
Identify **metaphors** and **similes** of concealment. How do they express Jekyll's confidence in the role of Hyde?

e **'Some two months … second and worse.'**
Identify questions expressing confusion. What do they suggest about the danger of losing control?

f **'Between these two … assaults of temptation.'**
How are metaphors used to express ideas about temptation and willpower?

Jekyll describes how even as a young man he felt that there were two sides to his nature: one serious and responsible and the other inclined to pleasurable pursuits.

He began experimenting with chemicals to separate the two sides of his personality and transformed himself into the person he called Edward Hyde.

As Hyde, he could do bad things freely. Jekyll told his servants that Hyde could visit his house. He named Hyde in his will and rented a house and set up a bank account in his name. As Hyde's actions grew worse, Jekyll started to hate him.

He was terrified one day when he turned into Hyde without taking the concoction. He eventually found that he needed more and more of the drug to stay in the shape of Jekyll. After murdering Carew while he was Hyde, he resolved to lead a good life as Jekyll.

While out one day, he turned into Hyde again without warning. Jekyll could not return home for his drug because Hyde was wanted for Carew's murder, so instead he came up with a plan for Lanyon to get the drug. From then on, he battled to keep his identity as Jekyll. Things got worse when he could no longer obtain the chemicals.

He wrote this letter to Utterson as Jekyll after taking his final dose of the drug, knowing that he would soon change into Hyde. He questioned whether he would be found and hanged or whether he would have the courage to commit suicide. Sealing this confession and awaiting his transformation ended his life as Henry Jekyll.

PUTTING DETAILS TO USE

The structure of a mystery

Stevenson makes Jekyll's statement **authentic** by including references that explain or confirm details from earlier in the story.

1 Work in small groups. Imagine that you are preparing evidence for an inquest into Jekyll's death. The coroner has read Jekyll's statement and asked you to supply information to help confirm the points identified in the grid.

    a Take a few of these points each. Read about them in Jekyll's statement, and then find relevant quotations and information in the chapters indicated.

    b Prepare a presentation for the inquest to show how other witnesses and events support what Jekyll has written.

Learning checkpoint

What do you think about *The Strange Case of Dr Jekyll and Mr Hyde*? Write at least three paragraphs explaining your personal response to the story. Make sure that you include:

✔ the extent to which you enjoyed it

✔ your opinion on how successful Stevenson is in constructing the plot

✔ your thoughts on the ideas that the story explores

✔ details from the text to support your comments and interpretations.

Find out more about plot and structure in the novel in Unit 11.

Jekyll acquired a mirror for his room. (Chapter 8)

Jekyll opened a bank account in Hyde's name. (Chapter 4)

He stuck to his resolution to stay as Jekyll for two months. (Chapter 6)

He employed a suitable housekeeper for the house he rented in Hyde's name. (Chapter 4)

Jekyll told his servants that Hyde was free to visit his house. (Chapter 2)

Hyde wrote blasphemies in religious books. (Chapter 8)

Jekyll became smaller when he changed into Hyde. (Chapters 2, 4 and 8)

Jekyll describes Carew's murder from Hyde's point of view. (Chapter 4)

Even when he was Hyde, his handwriting was still Jekyll's own. (Chapter 9)

When in the role of Hyde, Jekyll noticed that other people found his presence disturbing. (Any chapter in which other characters meet Hyde)

Jekyll destroyed the key for the back door of his house which he used as Hyde by grinding it under his foot. (Chapter 8)

By the end, Jekyll was unable to get the drug he needed. (Chapter 8)

The symbolism of concealment

In exploring the **theme** of concealment, Stevenson may be suggesting that respectable people keep aspects of their lives secret for fear of losing their reputation or place in society.

 1 Use a dictionary to help you explain the underlined words in these quotations. What **connotations** do they share?

   a   'to shake and to pluck back that <u>fleshly vestment</u>'

   b   'to assume, like a <u>thick cloak</u>, that of Edward Hyde'

   c   'in my <u>impenetrable mantle</u>, the safety was complete'

   d   'The <u>veil</u> of self-indulgence'.

> ### 🔑 Key terms
>
> **connotations:** the implied meanings or associations of a word.

Ideas about identity and the relationship between Jekyll and Hyde

The novel shows that identity is a complex idea. The 'face' that people present to the outside world may conceal different aspects of their personality.

1 Jekyll explains why he wants to separate the two sides to his nature, saying: '**If each [...] could but be housed in separate identities, life would be relieved of all that was unbearable.**' What do you think he means by this?

2 Jekyll describes the freedom he felt when he transformed into Hyde. Explain how the metaphors in the following quotations create a sense of that freedom:

   a   '... so potently controlled and shook the very <u>fortress of identity</u>'

   b   '... shook the doors of <u>the prison-house of my disposition</u>.'

If each ... could but be housed in separate identities, life would be relieved of all that was unbearable.

Jekyll: Chapter 10

The grammar of identity

Eventually, Jekyll lives in such fear and hatred of Hyde that he sees him as a separate person. The complexity of his identity as both Jekyll and Hyde is shown when uses both a **first-person** and **third-person narrative**:

'I ran to the house in Soho, and […] destroyed my papers; thence I set out through the lamplit streets […] gloating on my crime […] still hearkening in my wake for the steps of the avenger. Hyde had a song upon his lips as he compounded the draught, and as he drank it, pledged the dead man.'

first person

third person

Jekyll: Chapter 10

1 What do you think these grammatical shifts show about:

   a   Jekyll's state of mind
   b   ideas about identity?

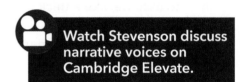

Watch Stevenson discuss narrative voices on Cambridge Elevate.

GETTING IT INTO WRITING

Writing about good and evil

1 Write a short essay on how the novel presents both the good and evil sides of human nature. Use this planning grid to help you to structure your answer.

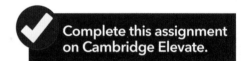

Complete this assignment on Cambridge Elevate.

Examples of the good aspects of human nature shown in the novel (Tip: consider Biblical references and charitable behaviour)	Examples of the evil aspects of human nature shown in the novel (Tip: refer to hypocrisy and selfishness in other characters as well as Jekyll)
Details of Stevenson's language in relation to goodness (Tip: look for links with Christianity)	Details of Stevenson's language in relation to evil (Tip: look for links with damnation, Hell and Satan, and metaphors of decay and corruption)
Conclude with a personal response: does the novel convince you that these two sides exist in human nature?	

GETTING FURTHER

Making links across the whole novel

1 Extend your understanding of the text as a whole by copying and completing the following table, adding details to help with revision.

 Key terms

third-person narrative: an account of events using 'he', 'she' or 'they', rather than 'I' or 'we'.

Chapter	Details to prompt your memory	Examples of these structural and language details	Key quotations
1. Story of the door	• Enfield's mystery about Hyde	• contrasts • emphasis on silence	
2. Search for Mr Hyde	• Jekyll's will • meet Lanyon • meet Hyde	• Utterson's questions and determination • nightmare description • animal imagery for Hyde • two sides of Jekyll's house	
3. Dr Jekyll was quite at ease	• first meet Jekyll	• dialogue between friends	
4. The Carew murder case	• murder • searching Hyde's rooms	• violent attack described • foggy journey	
5. Incident of the letter	• Jekyll is ill • Hyde escapes • letter from Hyde in Jekyll's writing	• fog • letter • forgery	
6. Remarkable incident of Doctor Lanyon	• Lanyon dies from shock	• precise dates • sealed document	
7. Incident at the window	• another Sunday walk • dramatic change in Jekyll	• symbol of window • realistic dialogue	
8. The last night	• Utterson called to Jekyll's house • he and Poole break the door down • Hyde dead • Jekyll disappeared	• disordered weather and servants • dialogue and social status • Jekyll's note to chemists • description of Hyde • dramatic action • package and sealed documents	
9. Dr Lanyon's narrative	• the revelation • events in letter from Jekyll • collects drawer full of chemicals • arrival of Hyde • transformation into Jekyll	• first-person narrative • scientific and medical language • dramatic revelation	
10. Henry Jekyll's full statement of the case	• early life and background to events • belief in duality • emotions, regret, despair	• first person narrative • covers all clues	

11

Plot and structure

How does Stevenson take his readers on a journey in the novel?

Your progress in this unit:
- ensure your understanding of the plot
- examine how narrative devices affect the reader's understanding and response to plot and structure
- explore how Stevenson creates suspense through the novel's structure.

THE STRUCTURE OF THE NOVEL

The Strange Case of Dr Jekyll and Mr Hyde is often referred to as a 'novella', which is a literary term for a work that is too long to be a short story, but shorter than a conventional novel.

Its ten chapters are uneven in length and vary in style. Stevenson uses them to create the impression of a legal or medical mystery, as the reader is guided through events by Mr Utterson. The 'Strange Case' in the title, and the style of the chapter headings – as though they come from a doctor's or detective's notes, or from a newspaper story – add to this impression. This approach creates realism and heightens the reader's interest and sense of anticipation.

Stevenson also makes the story seem like a realistic investigation by drawing attention to precise details of time. The action takes place over about 15 months, with most events happening during autumn and winter, providing a background of darkness and gloom.

THE PLOT OF THE NOVEL

Stevenson had considered writing about 'man's double being' for some time before the idea for *The Strange Case of Dr Jekyll and Mr Hyde* came to him. Apparently he had a dream about a scene at a window like the one in Chapter 7, and another one about a man taking a powder that transforms him. Stevenson developed the ideas in the novel from these dreams.

Choices about form and content

Stevenson consciously crafted his story – he made deliberate choices about the shape it should take and how it should be told. It is important to show that you understand how these choices affect the reader's response to the story. Think of the story in three sections:

- **Exposition:** Chapters 1–3
- **Development:** Chapters 4–7
- **Resolution:** Chapters 8–10.

Start by examining how Stevenson constructs the plot to heighten the suspense and the sense of horror. In Chapters 1–7, he sets out clues that intrigue and puzzle both Utterson and the reader, leaving them with questions to be answered.

Stevenson builds interest throughout the story, so the dramatic events at the end and the final 'big reveal' have a powerful impact. The ending provides an explanation, but it also raises questions about human nature.

WHO TELLS THE STORY?

The narrative voice

Stevenson creates various narrators, using **characters** to tell the story in their own voices through **dialogue** and written **testimony**. These different perspectives create an illusion of reality. The characters are lawyers and doctors – men of serious and reliable professions – so the reader trusts their accounts and judgements. However, think about what you learn about the characters as the novel progresses. Many of them reach the wrong conclusions or make wrong decisions. Do they know enough to be reliable narrators?

The effects of narrative devices

Stevenson writes in the third person to introduce Mr Utterson and describe his part in the story. Using a **third-person narrative** adds distance from the character – the reader is not inside Utterson's head but observes his actions as he investigates, prompted by the same clues and concerns that the reader has. This gives a realistic impression of a man who discovers something puzzling about the behaviour of a friend and looks into it fairly.

Personal testimony

The **first-person narrative** used in the accounts given by Lanyon and Jekyll creates a different effect and offers different perspectives on the **themes** in the novel. The first-person voice reveals the characters' thoughts, emotions and personal interests – and perhaps some **bias**. This is important, because it is the two men's different approaches to science that cause the breakdown in their friendship. Lanyon's horror at Jekyll's experiment brings about his death.

Look at the following extract, in which Lanyon shows his strong moral conviction and expresses a clear judgement of Jekyll:

> 'As for the moral turpitude that man unveiled to me, even with tears of penitence, I cannot, even in memory, dwell on it without a start of horror.'
>
> Lanyon: Chapter 9

Now look at this extract, in which the use of the first person gives the reader an insight into how Jekyll felt when he first transformed into Hyde:

> 'I felt younger, lighter, happier in body; within I was conscious of a heady recklessness.'
>
> Jekyll: Chapter 10

The importance of dialogue

Much of the story is told through dialogue: the conversations between characters. Stevenson uses this to further the plot in a realistic way. For example Utterson first hears of Hyde's actions from Mr Enfield, giving him information about the identity of the mysterious beneficiary in Jekyll's will.

 Key terms

exposition: the introduction or set-up of a story, including the main characters, the setting, plot and ideas.

resolution: the explanation at the end of a story, which ties up all the strands.

bias: a strong feeling for or against something.

DEVELOP AND REVISE

Understand the start, middle and end of the story

1 Copy and complete the following table, making notes in each column to remind yourself of details from Chapters 1–3 that set up the story.

Information about Utterson, Hyde and Jekyll	Impressions of the setting in Victorian London	Information about Dr Lanyon and Poole	Questions and a mystery that make Utterson take action	Hints at duality and deceptive appearances

2 Write a list of questions that need to be answered by the end of Chapter 3.

3 Summarise each of the following key events in Chapters 4–7 with two suitable quotations:

    a Hyde commits a brutal murder and Jekyll appears to cover up for him.
    b Dr Lanyon has a shock that kills him.
    c Jekyll starts a new life, which ends abruptly when he withdraws again.
    d Characters experience disturbing feelings of fear and horror.

4 Write a paragraph about how the events of Chapters 4–7 develop the plot.

5 Chapters 8–10 reveal the answer to the mystery in three stages:

- **Chapter 8:** Utterson discovers Hyde's dead body in Jekyll's room, but Jekyll has disappeared.
- **Chapter 9:** Dr Lanyon explains how Jekyll transformed into Hyde.
- **Chapter 10:** Jekyll explains what led to his discovery and transformation. He confesses his crimes and describes the two aspects of his personality.

In pairs, discuss the effects created by presenting the resolution in this way.

6 Which chapters end with a **cliff-hanger**? How does this affect the reader?

Describe the reader's response

1 Write three paragraphs describing the reader's response to each of the three sections of the novel. Try to use some of the following words.

shock	horror	pity	understanding
curiosity	anticipation	suspense	clarity
sympathy	tension	relief	expectation

Who says what?

1 Look at the following examples of different people's testimonies in the novel. For each one, write down which character provides it: Dr Jekyll, Mr Hyde, Dr Lanyon or Mr Enfield.

- a conversational account of an incident he witnessed
- b a holographic will
- c a letter announcing Hyde's escape
- d a note to a chemist
- e a horrific account of Jekyll's transformation into Hyde
- f a statement and confession.

2 Identify the information that Utterson gets from the conversations listed in the table, then explain what contribution each one makes to the plot. The first one has been done for you.

Write about plot and structure

1 Use your notes from this unit to help you answer the following question.

The Strange Case of Dr Jekyll and Mr Hyde **is a story of mystery and horror. Explain how Stevenson has made it successful. Write about:**

- **how he structures the story**
- **how the structure contributes to the suspense and sense of horror in the story.**

 Key terms

cliff-hanger: the end of a chapter when something surprising happens, so people will want to find out what happens next.

Utterson's conversation with …	Information	How it furthers the plot
Enfield during their Sunday walk	Hyde's trampling of the girl, his possession of a key to Jekyll's back door and a cheque signed by Jekyll.	It motivates Utterson to investigate Hyde and his link with Jekyll.
Lanyon in Chapter 2		
Hyde in Chapter 2		
Jekyll in Chapter 5		
Guest in Chapter 5		
Lanyon in Chapter 6		
Poole in Chapter 8		

'I felt younger, lighter, happier in body; within I was conscious of a heady recklessness.'

Jekyll: Chapter 10

12

Context and setting

How does Stevenson bring the setting and action alive?

Your progress in this unit:
- understand how the novel relates to its literary context
- explore Stevenson's presentation of settings
- understand how the novel reflects its social context.

ROBERT LOUIS STEVENSON

Stevenson's life

Stevenson was born in Scotland in 1850, the son of a successful civil engineer. He was brought up in the respectable professional middle class in Edinburgh. His childhood was shaped by poor health, which meant that he spent many of his early years in his bedroom. He was looked after by a religious nurse, who shared her Christian views with the young Stevenson. Her descriptions of the torments of Hell gave him nightmares, which continued to trouble him throughout his life.

In his twenties, Stevenson rejected the strict religious teaching of his upbringing, and quarrelled with his father about his views on religion. He also developed a more serious respiratory illness. The climate in Scotland did not suit him, so he spent much of his life abroad, eventually settling in Samoa.

Stevenson studied Law at Edinburgh University. However, he chose to pursue a career as a writer rather than as a lawyer. He wrote about his travels in Europe and elsewhere, but is best known for his fiction. The adventure story *Treasure Island* appeared in 1883 and was followed by *The Strange Case of Dr Jekyll and Mr Hyde* and *Kidnapped* (both 1886). Stevenson also wrote a stage adaptation of *Dr Jekyll and Mr Hyde* in 1888 and *The Master of Ballantrae* in 1889. He continued to write until his death in 1894.

Publication of *Dr Jekyll and Mr Hyde*

Stevenson was 35 when he wrote the novel, in October 1885. Although he had already gained fame with *Treasure Island*, he still needed financial support from his father. Stevenson claimed that he produced this story specifically to make money, and he wrote it at great speed – possibly in as little as three days. It was his first commercially successful book.

The story has remained popular ever since its publication. Adaptations for stage and film have made the idea of Jekyll and Hyde familiar to people who have not read the book, and the phrase 'Jekyll and Hyde personality' is widely used to suggest that someone leads a double life.

ROMANTICISM

Romanticism was a movement of ideas about art and literature that developed in the late 18th century, and which was at its peak from 1800 to 1850. Romanticism emphasises the importance of imagination, emotional self-expression and original ideas over order, self-control and rational ideas. It suggests that dreams and the natural world can give an insight into a person's soul. The influence of romanticism can still be seen in literature, film and television today.

Stevenson expresses **romantic** ideas in Jekyll's desire to release his inner self and **'spring headlong into the sea of liberty'**. His **'transcendental'**, **'unscientific'** interests contrast sharply with Lanyon's **rationalism**. Stevenson himself claimed that the story was inspired by a dream – and a dream appears in the novel as an expression of Utterson's deep anxieties.

Gothic literature

'Gothic' is a term used to describe a **genre** of romantic fiction that developed in the period 1790–1820. Its stories of horror and supernatural events were often set in distant countries and in long-ago, less-civilised times. The central figures in gothic stories were vulnerable heroines and aristocratic villains, and the stories were often set in ruined castles or haunted convents. Death, imprisonment and decay were popular **themes**. Later, gothic literature developed the vampire genre and the idea of the double or split identity.

Stevenson draws on the gothic tradition, but uses a 19th-century London **setting**. The intricate layout of Jekyll's house and its neglected laboratory replace the haunted castle, and the idea of imprisonment occurs in his body rather than in a prison cell. It is all the more thrilling that the darkness, fear and horror of Stevenson's story exist alongside everyday life.

THE LONDON SETTING

Although this is fiction, Stevenson makes London recognisable by mentioning familiar places. Hyde's house is in a seedy part of Soho – an area that his readers knew had a bad reputation. Dr Lanyon lives on Cavendish Square, described as **'that citadel of medicine'** because of the large number of doctors who lived and worked there. It emphasises his relationship with accepted medical practice. However, not every detail is precise and easily identifiable as London, and some readers have recognised features of Edinburgh in the story.

The key point is that Stevenson creates a convincing urban setting to bring the story closer to his readers' own lives. **Characters** travel through city streets, and the familiar nuisance of the London fog is never far away. The sense of horror is heightened by the suggestion that similar events could be happening **'down a bystreet in a busy quarter of London'**. Stevenson implies that the double standards and false appearances in the novel are much more common than his readers think.

Dr Jekyll's house

It is important to understand the details Stevenson gives about the location and 'geography' of Jekyll's house. He suggests duality even in the way he describes the square in which it stands:

Round the corner from the bystreet, there was a square of ancient, handsome houses, now for the most part decayed from their high estate and let in flats and chambers to all sorts and conditions of men: map-engravers, architects, shady lawyers, and the agents of obscure enterprises.

Chapter 2

There is a clear contrast here: the **adjectives** **'ancient'**, **'handsome'** and **'high'** suggest grandeur and respectability; **'decayed'**, **'shady'** and **'obscure'** show that the area has declined and that the business carried out there is secretive and possibly illegal. The contrasting front and back entrances are each associated with the two different lives of Jekyll and Hyde. The key for the rear door is an important **symbol** to remind the reader that Hyde is the embodiment of Jekyll's inner self, which has been 'unlocked' by the transforming potion.

 Key terms

rationalism: the idea of using knowledge and reason instead of belief or emotions as the basis for actions and opinions.

The story's link to real crimes

The Victorians had a great appetite for crime stories, in both newspapers and fiction, so the story of Jekyll and Hyde's deeds was well received. Stevenson shared their fascination. Growing up in Edinburgh, stories about strange crimes committed there fuelled his imagination and interest in horror. In 1820s Edinburgh, William Burke and William Hare killed people and supplied their bodies to a local surgeon. In another case that captured the public's imagination, William 'Deacon' Brodie led a double life for many years – by day he was a respected cabinet-maker but by night he burgled houses to pay for his gambling habit.

In a case of life appearing to imitate art, *The Strange Case of Dr Jekyll and Mr Hyde* was linked to the brutal Whitechapel murders committed in 1888, two years after the story was published. Detectives were unable to identify the murderer – known as Jack the Ripper – so there were many theories about his identity. At the time, a stage version of the novel was being performed in London, and its star, Richard Mansfield, briefly came under suspicion. People suggested that his convincing performance could encourage murder, and his transformation from Jekyll to Hyde on stage showed how effectively someone could conceal their identity.

DEVELOP AND REVISE

Understand contrasting points of view

1 Create a table like this. Add quotations to help you examine contrasting points of view in the novel.

Point of view	Chapter	Quotations
Utterson takes a rational approach to the search for Mr Hyde	2	'Utterson began to haunt the door […] at all hours […] the lawyer was to be found on his chosen post.'
	8	
Stevenson reveals Utterson's anxieties and inner thoughts in a dream	2	
Jekyll's view of Lanyon's opinions	3	
Lanyon's scientific observations	9	
Jekyll's exploration of his own inner thoughts	10	

Investigate the settings in the story

1 The settings are important in this novel, and Stevenson describes them at various points. Copy and complete the following table to help you gather together details on the key settings. Some examples have been given to get you started.

Setting	Key details, mood and atmosphere	Contribution to plot and character development	Themes and ideas associated with this setting
the street and door in Chapter 1			duality – the door is in sinister contrast to the street round the corner
the same street when Utterson sees Hyde in Chapter 2			
Jekyll's house in Chapter 2			
the setting for Carew's murder in Chapter 4	a peaceful, beautiful moonlit night	creates a calm atmosphere in contrast with the violent attack	good and evil – this innocent scene is ruined by Hyde's horrific behaviour
Utterson's journey with the Inspector to Soho in Chapter 4			
Hyde's house in Soho in Chapter 4		details add to the mystery around Hyde, making links with Jekyll	
Jekyll's house in Chapters 5 and 8			

Round the corner from the bystreet, there was a square of ancient, handsome houses, now for the most part decayed from their high estate

Chapter 2

13

Character and characterisation

How does Stevenson create memorable characters?

Your progress in this unit:
- understand the characters and their roles in the plot
- examine how Stevenson presents the characters
- understand how characters contribute to ideas in the novel.

All the main **characters** in *The Strange Case of Dr Jekyll and Mr Hyde* belong to the same narrow social group of doctors and lawyers. Stevenson **characterises** them as professional men with good reputations. Other men appear as minor characters to develop the story and to make it seem realistic. Very few female characters appear in the novel. Those that do are minor characters from lower social classes.

MR UTTERSON

Utterson's role in the plot

Stevenson uses Mr Utterson to reveal details of the story to the reader. Utterson is Jekyll's close friend and the lawyer who holds his will, so in Chapter 1 he is intrigued when Mr Enfield tells him about the incident involving Mr Hyde. His position in his group of friends and as a lawyer gives him authority and influence. Other characters respect him and ask for his help.

The result is that he is always close to the action and he asks the questions that the reader also wants answered. Following Utterson through the story, the reader shares his understanding of events and draws conclusions based on his judgement.

Characterisation of Utterson

Stevenson suggests Utterson's importance by introducing him first in the novel. The opening description contains contradictions about the character of Utterson that suggest he is a complex man: he appears '**austere**' and '**cold**' yet manages to be '**lovable**'. His main personal quality is '**tolerance for others**', and he was often the '**last reputable acquaintance and the last good influence in the lives of down-going men**'. These details suggest balance and lack of **bias**, qualities that make Utterson well suited to his role of investigator.

Stevenson shows Utterson fulfilling this role by asking questions and paying attention to details in pursuit of the truth. On the other hand, the reader understands that Utterson is not entirely open and honest. He frequently emphasises the importance of saying nothing or keeping silent, which may suggest that he is more concerned with maintaining people's reputations than with uncovering the truth.

Utterson's role in relation to ideas and themes

Utterson reflects the **themes** of duality and double standards in his own complex personality (see Unit 14 for more on these themes). Although he wants to find answers, his silences contribute to secrecy and concealment in the novel. His inability to explain the whole mystery is further evidence of the strange nature of a case that defies normal methods of investigation.

DR LANYON

Lanyon's role in the plot

Dr Lanyon's main role is as another narrator, when he writes his account of the horrifying transformation of Jekyll into Hyde. His **testimony** reveals this important aspect of the plot, which has been a puzzle for both the reader and Utterson until this point. Earlier in the novel, Stevenson uses Lanyon to raise questions and increase suspense when he describes the shocking change that leads to his death.

Characterisation of Lanyon

Stevenson uses language to emphasise that Lanyon is a doctor and a man who takes a scientific approach to life based on accepted knowledge. Lanyon presents a different perspective from Jekyll's. He calls Jekyll '**fanciful**' and his interests '**unscientific balderdash**'.

Lanyon's role in relation to ideas and themes

Lanyon's views and values are a direct contrast with Jekyll's. His shock at Jekyll's revelation is so strong that it kills him, leaving the reader with a powerful impression of horror. Like the other men, Lanyon is capable of acting a role that hides his true feelings.

DR JEKYLL AND MR HYDE

It is only in the final testimonies of Lanyon and Jekyll at the end of the story that Stevenson reveals that Jekyll and Hyde are the same person. Lanyon explains how he witnessed the dramatic transformation. Jekyll explains how he experimented to find a way to separate the two parts of himself so that the evil side of his nature could pursue its pleasures without being troubled by the conscience of its better half. Jekyll refers to '**my original and better self**' and '**… my second and worse**'.

MINOR CHARACTERS

Although the following characters play only a small part, their contributions to the plot and the reader's understanding of the main characters is important.

Mr Enfield

Enfield's contribution to the plot comes at the start, when he tells Utterson about the incident with Hyde and the door. Although he appears only briefly, Stevenson provides enough information about Enfield to make him relevant to the novel's themes and ideas. He is the first one to express the idea of keeping quiet: '**The more it looks like Queer Street, the less I ask.**'

There is another hint of secrets when Enfield only vaguely accounts for his presence on the street at three o'clock in the morning, saying: '**I was coming home from some place at the end of the world**', without being specific. Perhaps he is another respectable man with secrets to hide.

 Key terms

characterise: to describe features that are unique or distinctive.

Poole

Jekyll's butler is shown as the loyal servant who is familiar with his master's life and protective of his reputation. His language is respectful, matching his place in society. He contributes to the plot by supplying important information to Mr Utterson – first about not receiving delivery of a letter in Chapter 5, and then about Jekyll's behaviour in Chapter 8.

Mr Guest

Mr Guest is Utterson's head clerk, and an amateur expert in the science of handwriting. It is he who notices the similarity between Hyde's and Jekyll's writing, leading Utterson to suspect Jekyll of forging for a murderer.

Hyde's housekeeper

Stevenson makes the housekeeper well-suited to working for Hyde. She has a face 'smoothed by hypocrisy' and 'excellent manners', emphasising once again that things are not what they seem.

The maidservant

This 'romantically given' young woman witnesses Carew's murder. The language of her testimony creates a strong contrast between the innocent victim and the evil murderer.

DEVELOP AND REVISE

Explore Utterson's character

1 Find short quotations from Utterson's speeches that show the contrasting aspects of his character. You might like to start by looking at his conversations with Jekyll in Chapters 5 and 7.

2 Identify at least three occasions on which Utterson expresses the importance of saying nothing. Start by reading the end of his conversations with Enfield and Guest, and his words to Poole at the end of Chapter 8.

Explore Lanyon's character

1 Analyse how the language in the following extract from Lanyon's narrative reveals his scientific background and methods:

'… a simple crystalline salt of a white colour. The phial, to which I next turned my attention, might have been about half-full of a blood-red liquor, which was highly pungent to the sense of smell and seemed to me to contain phosphorus and some volatile ether.'

Lanyon: Chapter 9

Explore Jekyll and Hyde

1 Look at the word bank. What evidence can you find in the novel to support each word or phrase about Dr Jekyll?

outwardly respectable
popular
charitable works
deceitful
duality of human nature
untroubled conscience
weak-willed

2 Now look at this word bank and find evidence for each word or phrase to describe Mr Hyde.

> physically small
>
> deformed
>
> evil nature
>
> effect on others
>
> animal-like
>
> violent actions
>
> does not fit into polite society

3 Summarise what you have learnt by writing notes on how Stevenson presents Jekyll and Hyde. Copy the following spider diagram as your starting point, then add to it.

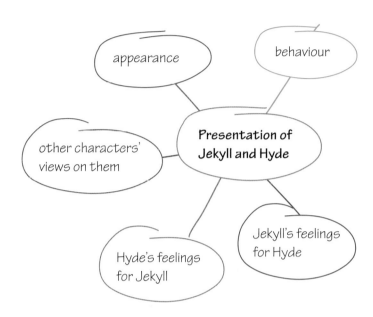

appearance

behaviour

other characters' views on them

Presentation of Jekyll and Hyde

Hyde's feelings for Jekyll

Jekyll's feelings for Hyde

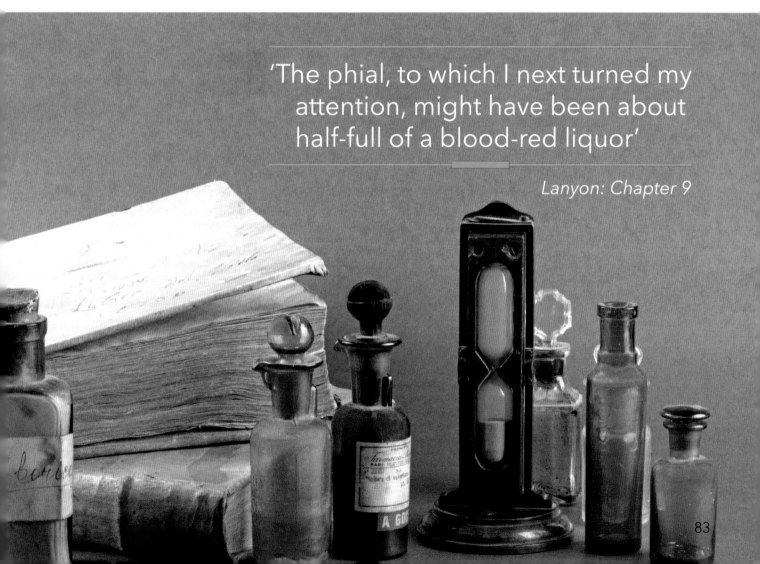

'The phial, to which I next turned my attention, might have been about half-full of a blood-red liquor'

Lanyon: Chapter 9

14

Themes and ideas

What big ideas dominate the novel?

MAJOR THEMES IN THE NOVEL

Stevenson explores ideas through the **characters**, events and **settings** he describes, and these occur as **themes** throughout the novel.

Duality – two sides to everything

Think about duality in relation to the following elements in the novel, and then add to the list with examples of your own:

Setting:

- Victorian London
- Soho itself
- Jekyll's house.

Characterisation:

- Utterson's characterisation
- Jekyll's characterisation
- Jekyll versus Hyde.

Perspectives:

- Jekyll versus Lanyon.

Secrecy and concealment

Stevenson explores this theme throughout the novel. The main plot is concerned with uncovering the mystery of Hyde's actions and identity, and the secrets that Jekyll appears to be hiding. Words that suggest covering up, such as '**cloak**', '**veil**', '**mantle**' and '**mask**', are used in relation to Jekyll in his role as Hyde.

There are also many hints of secrecy concerning other characters, and these lead the reader to consider ideas about **hypocrisy**. Characters avoid sharing information, preferring to keep silent and protect reputations. Dr Lanyon will not talk about his disagreement with Jekyll. No explanation is given about why Mr Enfield and Sir Danvers Carew are walking around London at the dead of night. Even at the end, with Hyde's dead body on the floor and Jekyll nowhere to be seen, Utterson advises Poole: '**I would say nothing of this paper. If your master has fled or is dead, we may at least save his credit.**'

Stevenson uses physical settings and descriptive details to increase the sense of secrecy. Think about the atmosphere and setting of the novel, the times of day things happen and the different ways that characters struggle to see things clearly, or are blocked from finding things out. What recurring **symbols** or **metaphors** can you identify that Stevenson uses?

Good and evil

Jekyll's experiment is based on his belief that man's good and evil sides are equally valid aspects of his identity. The two sides, '**good and ill, divide and compound man's dual nature**'. They 'divide' because the two parts are separate and conflicting; they 'compound' because together they make up the whole person. He believes it is '**the curse of mankind**' that the two are bound together.

Stevenson makes Hyde come across as violent and merciless – Carew's mild enquiry results in a violent attack. Stevenson presents it in the kind of detail that might be seen in a sensational news report, using the violent verbs '**clubbed**' and '**trampling**'. He gives vivid details of the effects of the attack: '**the bones were audibly shattered and the body jumped upon the roadway**'.

All the characters who meet Hyde are disturbed by the sense of evil that surrounds him. Stevenson's technique of repeating this idea without being specific encourages the reader to imagine the worst. The maid can say only that Hyde was '**particularly small and particularly wicked-looking**'. This reflects ideas that were popular at the time that appearances reflected someone's true personality. The same idea is suggested when Jekyll writes: '**Evil […] had left on that body an imprint of deformity and decay**.'

 Key terms

hypocrisy: the pretence of having higher moral values than is really the case.

'Man is not truly one, but truly two.'

Jekyll: Chapter 10

Christian views of good and evil

Characters' perceptions of good and evil are shaped by Christian values. Hyde is associated with Christian ideas about Hell and Satan. He shows no mercy or regret. Jekyll calls him '**the spirit of Hell**' and '**my devil**'.

The language of Christianity provides a moral framework for the novel. Stevenson shows this through **allusions** to Christian belief and values. For example Utterson responds '**Amen**' when Poole calls on God's help, and when Jekyll starts a new life he became '**distinguished for religion**'.

Temptation

Stevenson does not say exactly what Jekyll's secret desires and pleasures are, but his 19th-century readers might have understood this to mean some sort of sexual crime. In large cities, crime and wrongdoing existed alongside respectable life. People were expected to resist temptation and uphold moral and religious standards as an example to others.

Although Hyde '**alone in the ranks of mankind was pure evil**', and you have considered Jekyll and Hyde in the context of duality already, it is worth asking yourself whether you think Stevenson presents Jekyll as a wholly good character. Here are some questions to think about. Find short quotations or examples from the text to support your answers.

- Why does Jekyll create Hyde in the first place?
- Does Jekyll enjoy being Hyde?
- Are Hyde's actions his own, or are they really Jekyll's?
- How did Hyde get so much stronger than Jekyll?

At the end, Jekyll regrets letting Hyde out. His last act as the doctor is to commit suicide so he does not have to live on as Hyde with no hope of changing back into his 'respectable' self.

Animal instincts

Hyde is often described with animal characteristics. He is said to '**hiss**' and '**snarl**'. Witnesses describe him as '**ape-like**', and he is frequently referred to as a '**creature**'. Hyde represents the '**lower elements**' of Jekyll's character.

These details should be considered in the **context** of Charles Darwin's book, *On the Origin of Species*, which was published in 1859. This book introduced the theory of evolution – the idea that all species evolved from simple life forms by the process of natural selection, in which those best suited to their environment would survive and pass on their characteristics. Some people were concerned by the link Darwin made between humans and animals. If evolution meant progress and improvement, perhaps the opposite could also happen – there could be a process of 'devolution', where people would revert to animal behaviour.

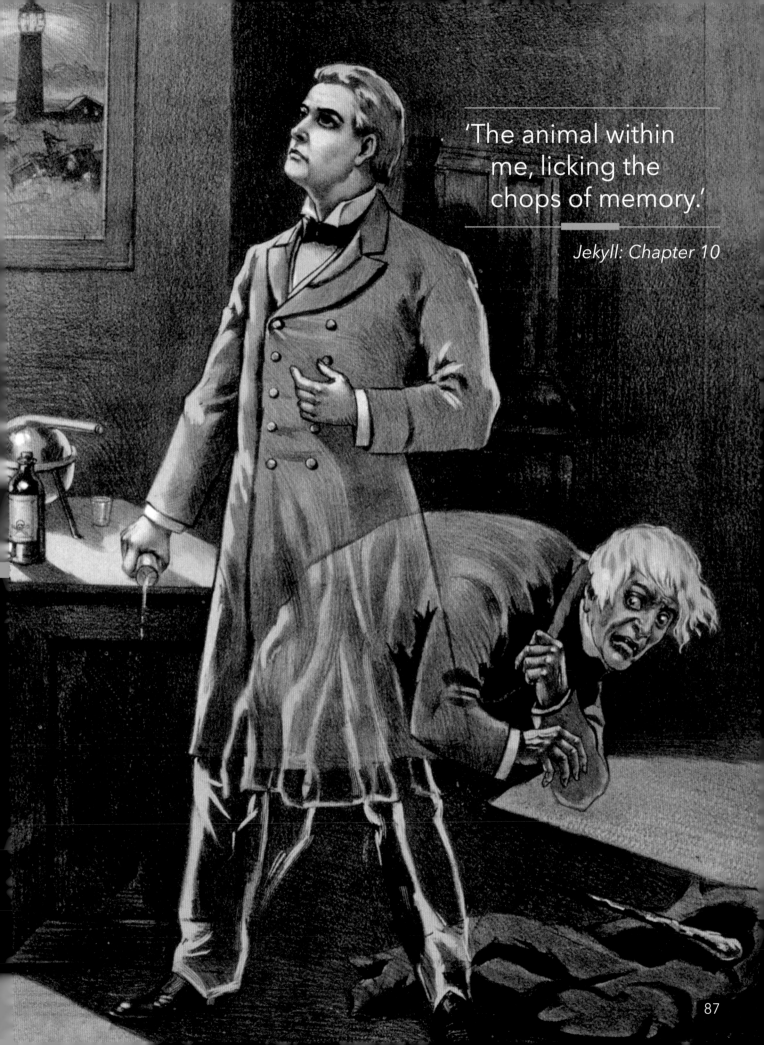

'The animal within me, licking the chops of memory.'

Jekyll: Chapter 10

In *The Strange Case of Dr Jekyll and Mr Hyde*, Hyde's animal qualities – his hairy hands, his strength and his appetite for dubious pleasures – reflect these ideas.

By the time the novel was published, many people were arguing that 'civilisation' should enable humans to overcome and contain their animal instincts. Through Jekyll, Stevenson shows that the civilising influences of religion, education and professional friends were not always successful.

Medicine and science

Darwin's work is just one example of the changes in scientific understanding that took place in the 19th century. It was a period of advancement based on rational thought. Stevenson presents Dr Lanyon as a rational scientist who observes details and seeks scientific proof. Importantly, he falls out with Jekyll over his 'unscientific' ideas. Later, Hyde taunts Lanyon for being '**bound to the most narrow and material views**' and denying '**the virtue of transcendental medicine**'.

Jekyll's approach is a more **romantic** one than Lanyon's. He places the individual and spiritual above society and reason. His experiment releases the emotions and instincts that his scientific discipline had kept in check.

Early in the 19th century, it was only legal to dissect the bodies of criminals who had been hanged. Surgeons who obtained corpses legally would perform dissections in front of an audience of other scientists or anatomy students. However others obtained them illegally. Stevenson explains that the outbuilding at Jekyll's house was:

… indifferently known as the laboratory or the dissecting-rooms. The doctor had bought the house from the heirs of a celebrated surgeon.

Chapter 5

This would have signalled something sinister to 19th-century readers. Indeed, Mr Utterson '**eyed the dingy, windowless structure with curiosity, and gazed round with a distasteful sense of strangeness as he crossed the theatre**', even though Jekyll was experimenting with chemicals rather than dissecting body parts.

Science could be both wonderful and terrifying. People might see its benefits in real life, but only the educated classes would understand it. Stevenson presents the wonder of science in his descriptions of Jekyll's chemical processes. But the novel might also be read as a warning of the dangers of experimenting with drugs, especially if they allow animal instincts to come to the surface.

DEVELOP AND REVISE

Explore the themes of duality and secrecy

You need to know where the themes of duality and secrecy/concealment occur, but you also need to be able to interpret the conclusions that Stevenson draws about them.

1 Consider the themes of duality and of secrecy/concealment. What conclusions do you think Stevenson draws about them? Write a paragraph in response to each of the following prompts.

   a How does Stevenson present ideas about duality in the novel? (Look at the two sides of Utterson's personality and the contrast between the street with the sinister door and the neighbouring streets in Chapter 1. Then identify other examples in the other chapters.)

   b Does the writer convince you that everything has two sides?

   c Do you think he suggests that this is a good or bad thing? Give reasons for your answers.

2 Write about your response to the theme of secrecy and concealment in a similar way.

    a   How does Stevenson present ideas about this theme in the novel?

    b   Does the novel criticise people for hiding aspects of their lives and behaviour? Find evidence from the text to support your answer.

    c   Do you think Utterson is right or wrong not to enquire too deeply but just to maintain his '**approved tolerance for others**'?

Explore the theme of good and evil

1 The theme of good and evil is closely linked to ideas about duality and secrecy. Write down your thoughts about the following statements, making sure you support your point of view with details from the text.

    a   The novel shows that we face a continuous struggle between good and evil.

    b   Society forces people to hide their true selves.

    c   The meaning of evil changes according to different contexts.

    d   Good and evil are shown in people's appearances.

    e   The good part of Jekyll's nature won through in the end.

Connect themes

1 Because themes and ideas are **abstract**, it can be difficult to fully explain how they are represented in the novel. It helps to connect them to something **concrete** and specific. Copy and complete the following table to show where different themes occur in the novel, and the characters connected with them. Then add more examples.

 Key terms

abstract: describing things that exist only as ideas.

concrete: describing things that exist in physical form.

Theme	Details of where it occurs: event, place characters	Quotation	Ideas this example expresses about the theme
duality			
secrecy and concealment			
good and evil			
animal instincts			
science and medicine			

15

Language

Why does the language have such impact?

Your progress in this unit:
- explore the language Stevenson uses to create meaning and effects
- explore the presentation of characters through language.

SENTENCE STRUCTURES

Everything that Stevenson does in the novel is done through language. Narrative, **characterisation**, mood, **settings** and ideas are all conveyed through the writer's choice of words and the ways he structures his sentences.

Driving the narrative and action

In Jekyll's final statement, he describes the first time he mixed his potion in a long paragraph that begins, '**I hesitated long before I put this theory to the test**'. Each phrase in this sentence describes a separate part of the process: Jekyll '**compounded [mixed] the elements**', boiled the mixture, watched it '**smoke**' and then subside, before drinking it.

By putting all the information into a single sentence, Stevenson suggests that Jekyll's actions were unstoppable – once he started, he had no choice but to continue. He also builds suspense by putting the most important action at the very end. All the details earlier in the sentence are about the scientific process, which heightens the suspense leading up to the point where Jekyll '**drank off the potion**'. This identifies it as a significant moment, preparing the reader for an account of what happened next.

Delaying the revelation of crucial information in this way creates appropriate effects in a mystery story. Look at another example:

> complex sentence

> phrase describing the setting

'But the hand which I now saw, clearly enough, in the <u>yellow light of a mid-London morning</u>, lying half shut on the bed-clothes, was <u>lean, corded, knuckly, of a dusky pallor and thickly shaded</u> with a swart growth of hair. <u>It was the hand of Edward Hyde.</u>'

Jekyll: Chapter 10

> simple sentence confirms reader's suspicions and Jekyll's fear

> intensifies the sense of horror and hints at what has happened

> phrase describing the hand

With the description of the hand, the reader starts to guess what has happened, knowing that these details match earlier descriptions of Hyde. The second sentence states starkly the terrible position Jekyll is in.

Revealing emotions and states of mind

Both Jekyll and Lanyon reveal their emotions and states of mind in their personal **testimonies**. Stevenson's choice of sentence structures help to do this effectively.

When describing how Jekyll was unable to shake off the sensations of becoming Hyde in Chapter 10, for example, Stevenson repeatedly uses the phrase '**in vain**' to emphasise Jekyll's anguish. Later in the chapter, Stevenson shows Jekyll's confusion and loss of control by his desperate self-questioning.

LANGUAGE IN THE NOVEL

Language to present people

Stevenson's language shapes how readers respond to **characters** in the novel. He chooses words carefully for their **connotations** in order to reveal information about a character's mood, actions and relationships. In this extract, for example, Jekyll uses the **metaphor** of a prison. He writes that the drug:

simile

other words suggesting imprisonment extend the metaphor

'… shook the doors of the <u>prison-house</u> of my disposition; and <u>like the captives</u> of Philippi, that which stood within ran forth. At that time my virtue slumbered; my evil, kept awake by ambition, <u>was alert and swift to seize the occasion</u>; and the thing that was projected was Edward Hyde.'

Jekyll: Chapter 10

personifies the evil aspect of Jekyll's nature

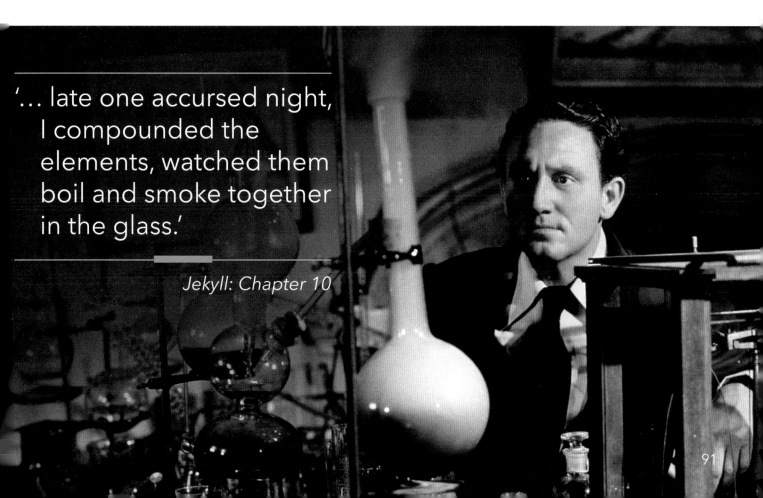

'… late one accursed night, I compounded the elements, watched them boil and smoke together in the glass.'

Jekyll: Chapter 10

It is important to be able to explain why Stevenson's metaphors work well. For example the metaphor of imprisonment is very effective here. It suggests that something is being repressed or held in. People in prison are often desperate to escape, so the **simile** is a good way of expressing how eagerly Jekyll's evil side came out. This is emphasised by the idea of speed in the words '**ran**' and '**swift**'.

In describing the relationship between Jekyll and Hyde, Stevenson uses the simile that Hyde remembered Jekyll '**as the mountain bandit remembers the cavern in which he conceals himself from pursuit**'. This reminds the reader of Hyde's criminal interests. Extending this idea with the word '**cavern**' shows that Hyde thinks of Jekyll simply as shelter rather than as a human being.

Language to present places and settings

Stevenson's descriptions create atmosphere and help the reader to understand ideas associated with the characters. Towards the end of his 'statement' in Chapter 10, Jekyll describes the atmosphere on a January day in London's Regent's Park. **Adjectives** such as '**clear**', '**fine**', '**cloudless**' and '**sweet**' create a mood of ease and relaxation. The onomatopoeic '**chirrupings**' sounds like pleasant birdsong and appeals to the sense of hearing. '**Spring odours**' appeals to the sense of smell. Stevenson wants the reader to feel Jekyll's mood at this point. Jekyll's false sense of security makes his sudden, involuntary transformation into Hyde a few moments later even more horrifying.

Language forms for realistic voices

Stevenson makes the characters' **dialogue** seem more realistic by imitating the structures of natural speech. When they are emotional or uncertain, the characters speak less fluently. In this example, Poole keeps hesitating to explain or correct himself:

'It was sometimes his way — the master's, that is — to write his orders on a sheet of paper and throw it on the stair … Well, sir, every day, ay, and twice and thrice in the same day …'

Poole: Chapter 8

DEVELOP AND REVISE

Explore sentence structures

1 Design a checklist like the following to highlight important features of sentences in the text. Add examples to illustrate each feature. Make notes on how each example affects the reader's understanding.

Sentence structure/feature	Examples from the novel	How it affects the reader's understanding
short statements		
questions		
repeated phrases		
hesitation		
exclamation		
long descriptive sentences		

Investigate figurative language

1 Identify some examples of Stevenson's figurative language, then put them in a table like this, explaining how the language choices shape the reader's understanding of events.

Figurative language	Example quotations	Type of figurative language	How the language choices shape the reader's understanding
animal references in relation to Hyde			
doors, windows, locks and seals			
fog		metaphor	

Preparing for your exam

WHAT THE EXAM REQUIRES

For your GCSE in English Literature, you will be assessed on *The Strange Case of Dr Jekyll and Mr Hyde* in **Section B** of **Paper 1: Shakespeare and the 19th-century novel**. You will have 1 hour and 45 minutes, and it is worth 40% of your GCSE in English Literature. You have just over 50 minutes for your answer on *The Strange Case of Dr Jekyll and Mr Hyde*.

You will have to answer one question on *The Strange Case of Dr Jekyll and Mr Hyde*. You will be required to write in detail about an extract from the novel that is printed on your exam paper and then to write about the novel as a whole. The question is worth 30 marks.

The first part of the question will make clear the part of the text provided, and the subject to be focused on. Then there will be two bullet points, emphasising that the answer should be based on the extract and on the novel as a whole.

The format of the question is like this:

In an extract from (Chapter X) Stevenson describes (person, situation, event, place, relationship, emotions, etc.). Write about:

- **how Stevenson presents the (person, situation, event, place, relationship, emotions, etc.) in that extract**
- **how the (person, situation, event, place, relationship, emotions, etc.) are presented in the novel as a whole.**

The assessment objective skills

Your answers will be assessed against three assessment objectives (AOs) – skills that you are expected to show. Notice the marks for each assessment objective and take account of this as you manage your time and focus your response.

- **AO1:** Read, understand and write about what happens in the novel, referring to the text and using relevant quotations. (12 marks)
- **AO2:** Analyse the language, form and structure used by Stevenson to create meanings and effects. (12 marks)
- **AO3:** Show an understanding of the context of the novel. This might include, depending on the question, when Stevenson wrote the novel, the period in which he set the novel and why it was set then, its relevance to readers then and to you in the 21st century. (6 marks)

Read the practice question and the annotations.

The Strange Case of Dr Jekyll and Mr Hyde

Read the following extract from Chapter 2 of *The Strange Case of Dr Jekyll and Mr Hyde* and then answer the question that follows.

> *In this extract, Mr Utterson has just met Mr Hyde for the first time.*
>
> 'We have common friends,' said Mr Utterson.
>
> 'Common friends?' echoed Mr Hyde, a little hoarsely. 'Who are they?'
>
> 'Jekyll, for instance,' said the lawyer.
>
> 'He never told you,' cried Mr Hyde, with a flush of anger. 'I did not think you would have lied.'
>
> 'Come,' said Mr Utterson, 'that is not fitting language.'
>
> The other snarled aloud into a savage laugh; and the next moment, with extraordinary quickness, he had unlocked the door and disappeared into the house.
>
> The lawyer stood awhile when Mr Hyde had left him, the picture of disquietude. Then he began slowly to mount the street, pausing every step or two and putting his hand to his brow like a man in mental perplexity. The problem he was thus debating as he walked was one of a class that is rarely solved. Mr Hyde was pale and dwarfish; he gave an impression of deformity without any nameable malformation, he had a displeasing smile, he had borne himself to the lawyer with a sort of murderous mixture of timidity and boldness, and he spoke with a husky whispering and somewhat broken voice; all these were points against him, but not all of these together could explain the hitherto unknown disgust, loathing and fear with which Mr Utterson regarded him. 'There must be something else,' said the perplexed gentleman. 'There *is* something more, if I could find a name for it. God bless me, the man seems hardly human! Something troglodytic, shall we say? or can it be the old story of Dr Fell? or is it the mere radiance of a foul soul that thus transpires through, and transfigures, its clay continent? The last, I think; for, O my poor old Harry Jekyll, if ever I read Satan's signature upon a face, it is on that of your new friend.'

Starting with this extract, how does Stevenson present Mr Hyde as a frightening outsider? Write about:

- how Stevenson presents Mr Hyde in this extract
- how Stevenson presents Mr Hyde as a frightening outsider in the novel as a whole.

[30 marks]

Annotations (margin notes):

- Dialogue. Mr Utterson polite and reasonable contrasts with Hyde's angry response.
- Narrative. Hyde's mood is quick to anger.
- Word choice. Verb 'snarled' and adjective 'savage' sound animal-like and threatening.
- Comparison. Utterson is troubled by Hyde's appearance and behaviour.
- Alliteration emphasises violence.
- List of abstract nouns show Utterson's reaction to Hyde.
- Exclamations and questions. Utterson is confused and puzzled by Hyde.
- Shows Utterson's Christian attitude.
- Exclamation and adjective 'poor' show that Utterson fears the effect on Jekyll.
- Metaphor of Hell to express Hyde's evilness.
- Start with a close reference to the text in the printed extract before widening your response to the novel as a whole. (AO1, AO2)
- This asks you to include contextual elements (AO3). In this case, the topic is being a frightening outsider. You need to stick to this.
- You need to make some sort of judgement here.
- Focus on the writer and think about the text as created by Stevenson. (AO2)

Plan your answer

When planning your answer to any question, focus on three key areas:

- What do you know about the characters, events and ideas at this stage – in this extract and in the novel as a whole? (AO1)
- What comments can you make about how Stevenson uses language and style, using examples from this extract? (AO2)
- What is relevant in this extract that relates to the context of the novel as a whole? (AO3)

Look at this example of a student's plan, then explore the example paragraphs and development of skills in writing for GCSE English Literature that follow.

- Utterson's first view of Hyde make him fearful and uneasy.
- Vague details of Hyde's effect on Utterson add mystery.

- He has no friends or family.
- Poole views him as a 'creature'.
- Even Jekyll is frightened of him in the end.

- Hyde's violence in Enfield's story is frightening.
- He is brutal in Carew's murder.

Hyde as frightening outsider

- Language of religion suggests ideas of good and evil. Hyde belongs to Hell.

- Hyde's rudeness contrasts with Utterson's politeness.
- Animal imagery comments on Hyde's character and behaviour.

Is Hyde a frightening outsider? He is different, frightening and a threat to society, but he's no outsider because he's the hidden side of Jekyll's personality.

Remember:

- ✔ **The best answers** will explore Stevenson's craft and purpose in creating characters and relationships. They will connect what the characters do, and their relationships, to the writer's ideas and to the effects upon the reader. They offer a personal response and provide many well-explained details.
- ✔ **Good answers** will show a clear understanding of how Stevenson develops the character of Hyde and his relationships, using well-chosen examples.
- ✔ **Weaker answers** will only explain what Mr Hyde does without using many examples or mentioning how Stevenson presents him.

Show your skills

To help you think about your own writing, look at these six example paragraphs of writing about *The Strange Case of Dr Jekyll and Mr Hyde*. The annotations show the range of skills displayed in each paragraph.

Hyde is a bad person who shows the other side of Dr Jekyll. This is the first time we see him face to face, and he seems very frightening.

Some simple facts stated.

When Utterson approaches him, Hyde reacts unpleasantly with 'a flush of anger'. We see that he is frightening because he 'snarled' and gave a 'savage laugh'.

Statement supported with quotation.

Stevenson has presented Hyde so far as a violent and evil character. His threatening behaviour is seen here when he 'snarled' and gave a 'savage laugh'. This is the first time that Utterson meets Hyde and he thinks that Hyde has 'Satan's signature' on his face. This warns the reader that Hyde is frightening and dangerous, which is what we see in his behaviour later in the novel.

> Explanation structured by reference to writer, reader and other parts of the text.

Stevenson makes Hyde appear frightening by emphasising his animal characteristics when he 'snarled' and gave a 'savage laugh'. This makes him sound wild and dangerous. Utterson is disturbed by his manner and his 'murderous mixture of timidity and boldness'. As Utteron walks away, he feels 'disgust, loathing and fear' and worries about Hyde's effect on his friend Jekyll. Like Mr Enfield, Utterson makes a link between Hyde and Satan to show that he is evil.

> Provides a range of detail to keep clearly illustrating a point.

Utterson's meeting with Hyde conveys ideas of evil and mystery. Hyde is shown as a frightening creature when he 'snarled' and gave a 'savage laugh'. Utterson's puzzlement about his identity is shown when he thinks, 'the man seems hardly human!' and brings in the idea of a primitive caveman: 'something troglodytic'. Stevenson shows the conventional and polite Mr Utterson as a contrast to Hyde, and Hyde's difference is part of the mystery.

> Uses details to develop an interpretation, going beyond what the text states explicitly.

Through Utterson's meeting with Hyde, Stevenson brings in the idea of the contrast between good and evil. The reader already knows that Utterson is a respected lawyer who represents tolerance and humane values. In Hyde, he meets someone who leaves him with a feeling of 'disquietude' because of his 'flush of anger' and the animal characteristics of a 'savage laugh'. Stevenson uses Utterson to express a Christian point of view when he concludes that Hyde has a 'foul soul' and 'Satan's signature' on his face. Stevenson's 19th-century readers would have recognised these references to evil, and understood why Utterson fears the effect on his friend Jekyll of associating with Mr Hyde. The mystery that surrounds Hyde's relationship with Jekyll pushes Utterson on to investigate further.

> An argued interpretation that includes references to writer, contexts and ideas.

Plan and write your own response

Now plan and write your own response to the practice question. You can then assess your skills against the example responses that follow.

 Complete this assignment on Cambridge Elevate.

ASSESS YOUR SKILLS

The following extracts are from sample responses to the practice question. They provide examples of skills at different levels when writing for GCSE English Literature. Use these examples to assess your own skills in responding to the practice question, so that you know what you do well and can focus on areas to improve. As you read the responses, think about how far each example – and your own answer – is successful in:

* using details from the text to support what the students have written
* using details to build up an interpretation of a character or theme
* exploring Stevenson's use of language and structure as well as his intentions in writing the novel.

Student A

This is taken from early in Student A's response:

Mr Hyde is a <u>mysterious, heartless</u> man who has already <u>behaved violently by</u> <u>trampling a girl on the street</u>. No one could understand why <u>Jekyll wrote a cheque</u> to pay damages to the girl's family. Utterson wants to know more about him and his link with Jekyll, so he has waited for him outside <u>the rear door to Jekyll's</u> house. When Utterson speaks to him he '<u>snarled aloud</u>' and gave a '<u>savage laugh</u>', then went into the house using his own key.

> Expresses a response to Mr Hyde.

> Shows understanding of the story.

> Mentions important detail.

> Mentions significant detail.

> Selects appropriate quotations.

This is taken from further on in Student A's response:

Later on, Hyde shows an even worse side to his character when a housemaid sees him murder Sir Danvers Carew. His violence is frightening when he clubs the man to death with 'ape-like fury'. The maid recognises Hyde because he has visited the house where she works, but even so the police cannot track him down and he gets away with the murder. This is because he turns out to be Dr Jekyll in disguise so when he swallows the potion he changes back into Jekyll and no one can find him. At the end of the book Jekyll explains that Hyde is his evil side that he wanted to let out.

In these parts of the response, Student A engages with the character as a real person, rather than as a character created by the writer. The response shows:

- understanding of character, but not characterisation
- obvious textual detail to support simple comments on character and relationship
- awareness of the character's attitudes and feelings
- awareness of the character's development during the course of the novel
- awareness of settings and the link with the character.

1 Work in pairs. Annotate the second paragraph of Student A's answer to see if you can find more examples of the same skills, or any new ones.

2 Talk together about what you think is good about the answer.

3 Look carefully at the three assessment objectives. What advice would you give Student A on how to improve this answer?

Student B

This is taken from early in Student B's response:

Stevenson presents Hyde as a frightening character from the start by showing his violent nature and cruel actions. When Utterson meets him he responds for no reason 'with a flush of anger', and the words that Stevenson uses to describe his actions, 'snarled' and 'savage laugh', make him seem fierce and dangerous. His character is also shown by the effect he has on Mr Utterson, who regarded him with 'disgust, loathing and fear'. Stevenson conveys a sense of just how frightening he is by linking him with ideas about Hell when he uses the metaphor 'Satan's signature'.

Shows understanding of the writer's intentions.

Immediate focus on the question.

Uses well-chosen quotations to support a comment.

Discusses a second method of presentation.

Keeps focus on the question.

Accurate use of terminology.

This is taken from further on in Student B's response:

Later in the novel, Stevenson conveys an even stronger sense of fear around Hyde by describing his brutal murder of Sir Danvers Carew. The maid who witnesses it is so frightened that she faints. Other characters are physically affected by their feelings for Hyde. Poole reports that being in his presence made 'your marrow kind of cold and thin'. Even though this is not really possible, the metaphor shows how scary Hyde is. And also Lanyon is so horrified by what Jekyll has done that it kills him. By the end of the novel even Jekyll is afraid of the creature that he has let loose. In his statement he describes Hyde as 'pure evil'. When he realises that he can no longer control Hyde by using the potion, he decides that he has to commit suicide. Stevenson shows that Jekyll sees this as the only way of escaping that terrible part of himself.

This is a stronger response than Student A's. Student B is clearly focused on the author's craft and purpose. The response engages with character and ideas, and includes personal interpretation. It shows:

- understanding of Stevenson's characterisation
- carefully thought out comments on meaning of details from the text
- awareness of the effects of particular word choices, for example 'your marrow kind of cold and thin' as a metaphor for fear
- some exploration of Hyde's nature
- exploration of the characters' development and what they learn
- links between textual detail and the writer's ideas
- Hyde's relationships with others and how they fear him.

1 Work in pairs. Annotate the second paragraph of Student B's answer to see if you can find more examples of the same skills, or any new ones.

2 Talk together about what you think is good about the answer.

3 Look carefully at the three assessment objectives. What advice would you give Student B on how to improve this answer?

exam

...en from early in Student C's response:

This passage occurs before the answer to the mystery is revealed, so Stevenson uses it to increase the reader's understanding of Hyde's true nature. He presents Hyde as a character to be feared because, 'alone among men', he is 'pure evil'. Through Utterson's meeting with Hyde, Stevenson brings in the idea of the contrast between good and evil. The reader already knows that Utterson is a respected lawyer who represents tolerance and good values. Hyde leaves him with a feeling of 'disquietude' because of his 'flush of anger' and the animal characteristics of his 'savage laugh'. Stevenson also conveys an atmosphere of horror and fear in the novel by making links between Hyde and ideas about Hell. Stevenson expresses a Christian perspective that his 19th-century readers would be familiar with in Utterson's metaphor 'Satan's signature' to describe Hyde's appearance. Even readers today will recognise the hint of horror that this description contains. The novel contains many contrasts like this to emphasise ideas about the duality of man's nature. As Jekyll puts it, 'Man is not truly one but truly two'.

Annotations
Shows a good sense of the whole text.
Gives a sense of the writer's purpose.
Uses a quotation from elsewhere in the novel.
A confident link to ideas.
Shows understanding of context.
Uses correct terminology.
Shows awareness of the effect on the reader.
Considers different responses.
Refers to writer's technique.
Uses a key quotation to summarise the idea.

This is taken from further on in Student C's response:

Stevenson develops several ideas based on Hyde as a frightening character. He suggests that characters may be frightened of the truth that Hyde reveals about human nature. Dr Lanyon, for example, dies from shock at the horror of what Jekyll reveals to him. Characters are shown as hypocritical and keen to protect their respectable reputations. They may fear Hyde because he forces them to confront the evil inside themselves. Hyde's animal characteristics and 'ape-like' behaviour make people afraid because of the links they suggest with man's evolution from animals. At the time the novel was published, after Darwin's 'Origin of Species', some people feared that giving in to animal instincts might lead to human degeneration and the breakdown of civilised society. By making the evil side of Hyde so frightening, Stevenson has created a powerful horror story that makes the reader consider the scary idea that there might be a Hyde lurking inside everyone.

This is the best answer of the three student responses.

1 Comment on the ways in which Student C:

    a   understands what the extract is about – its ideas and importance in the novel

    b   explains the effect of the extract on the reader and shows why it has that effect

    c   uses quotations from the extract as evidence to support an argument and does not just put forward opinions without any support

    d   looks at the whole extract and does not get stuck on one part of it

    e   Shows a knowledge of the context in which the novel was written and how it might be received by 21st-century readers

    f   convincingly explores and evaluates one or more of the ideas in the text as a whole.

Practice questions

Use your learning in this section to create practice questions and develop your skills further.

1 Work with another student to:

a choose a topic from the list in this section, or another topic of your choice

b choose a suitable extract of around 300 words

c create your practice questions.

Use these prompts to create your question:

- Choose a suitable topic.
- Choose a suitable extract.
- Choose a focus for writing about the extract.

Your question should look like this:

Starting with this extract, write about how Stevenson presents (your choice of topic). Write about:

- **how Stevenson presents (your choice of focus) in this extract**
- **how Stevenson presents (your choice of focus) in the novel as a whole.**

Topics

- good and evil
- duality or double-sidedness
- respectability and hypocrisy
- a major character
- a minor character
- science and reason versus the imagination.

2 Now answer the question, using the skills you have developed. As you plan and write, think about how far you can show:

a a consistent focus on the question, always remembering never to just retell the plot

b your knowledge of the details of the novel by using direct quotations or references to the text if you cannot remember the quotations

c your understanding of a character, setting or theme

d your understanding of how Stevenson has used language and structure to create the novel

e your ideas about the context in which the novel was written and how readers in the 21st-century might react to it.

3 Swap work with your partner. Using these points and your work in this section, comment on the skills shown in the answer. Suggest three areas that could be improved.

 Complete this assignment on Cambridge Elevate.

Glossary

abstract describing things that exist only as ideas

adjective a word that describes a person, place or thing

allusion a reference to something that the listener or reader will recognise

authentic realistic and true to the character

bias a strong feeling for or against something

characterise to describe features that are unique or distinctive

characters the people in a story; even when based on real people, characters in a novel are invented or fictionalised

cliff-hanger the end of a chapter when something surprising happens, so people will want to find out what happens next

concrete describing things that exist in physical form

connotations the implied meanings or associations of a word

context the historical circumstances of a piece of writing, which affect what an author wrote and the way they wrote it

contrast to point out the ways in which two or more things are different from one another

dialogue a conversation between two or more people in a piece of writing

exposition the introduction or set-up of a story, including the main characters, the setting, plot and ideas

figuratively when language is used to describe or represent something – for example in a metaphor

first-person narrative an account of events using the pronouns 'I', 'me' and 'we'

genre the kind or type of literature to which a text belongs; stories within a particular genre will have similar characteristics

homophone a word that sounds the same as another word, but which has a different spelling and meaning, e.g. Hyde/hide

hypocrisy the pretence of having higher moral values than is really the case

idiomatic expression a creative phrase that people who speak the same language will understand (e.g. to 'make a clean breast of something' means to confess what you have done)

imagery language intended to conjure up a vivid picture in the reader's mind

irony an extra layer of meaning in something, so a reader understands more than the characters involved

metaphor a type of comparison that describes one thing as if it was another

onomatopoeia words that sound like the sounds they describe

oxymoron a figure of speech where contradictory words are put together to create a complex effect

pathetic fallacy the idea that the natural world is sympathetic to people's experiences and feelings – for example using fog to suggest that it is difficult to see matters clearly

personification a type of metaphor that gives human qualities to inanimate objects

pun a play on words; the use of a word or phrase with a double meaning

rationalism the idea of using knowledge and reason instead of belief or emotions as the basis for actions and opinions

resolution the explanation at the end of a story, which ties up all the strands

rhetorical question a question intended to make a point rather than requiring an answer.

romantic ideas in literature based on the part that human instincts, imagination and emotions play in a person's identity

sensual appeal describing writing that appeals to a reader's senses, such as sight and hearing

setting the description of the place in which a story is set

simile a comparison between two things that uses the words 'as' or 'like'

symbol an object used to represent something else

testimony an account given by a witness to an event

theme an idea that a writer keeps returning to, exploring it from different perspectives

third-person narrative an account of events using 'he', 'she' or 'they', rather than 'I' or 'we'

Acknowledgements

Picture credits

cover Oliver Burston/Alamy; p. 5 (t) Marilyn Kingwill/ArenaPAL/Topfoto; p. 5 (b) Old Paper Studios/Alamy; p. 7 AF Archive/Alamy; p. 9 World History Archive/Alamy; pp. 10–11 Donald Cooper/Photostage; p. 12 George Kuna/Fotolia; p. 13 Nejron Photo/Fotolia; p. 15 The Art Archive/Alamy; p. 18 Anna-Mari West/Fotolia; p. 19 Brian Jackson/Fotolia; p. 23 ITV/Rex Features; p. 24 Justinb/Fotolia; p. 25 jcavale/Fotolia; p. 27 Donald Cooper/Photostage; p. 28 Demian/Fotolia; p. 29 World History Archive/Alamy; p. 31 tab62/Fotolia; p. 34 Minerva Studio/Fotolia; p. 35 London Weekend Television/Rex Features; p. 37 World History Archive/Alamy; p. 40 peterzsuzsa/Fotolia; p. 41 Szabolcs Szekeres/Fotolia; p. 45 Marilyn Kingwill/ArenaPAL/Topfoto; p. 46 Michael Spring/Fotolia; p. 47 Victor Watts/Alamy; p. 49 The Print Collector/Alamy; p. 50 felix/Fotolia; p. 51 The Print Collector/Alamy; p. 53 Ig0rZh/Fotolia; p. 55 Mary Evans Picture Library/Alamy; p. 58 Mary Evans Picture Library/Fotolia; p. 59 North Wind Picture Archives/Alamy; p. 61 World History Archive/Alamy; p. 63 Marilyn Kingwill/ArenaPAL/Topfoto; p. 66 Photos12/Alamy; p. 67 D.R. Knock/Topfoto; p. 69 Donald Cooper/Photostage; p. 72 Sergey Yarochkin/Fotolia; p. 75 AF Archive/Alamy; p. 76 Photos12/Alamy; p. 79 Douglas Freer/Fotolia; p. 80 Photos12/Alamy; p. 80 Francesca Marvulli/Fotolia; p. 83 Francesca Marvulli/Fotolia; p. 84 haitaucher39/Fotolia; p. 85 Mary Evans Picture Library/Alamy; p. 87 GL Archive/Alamy; p. 90 Donald Cooper/Photostage; p. 91 Snap/Rex Features; p. 94 Interfoto/Alamy.

Produced for Cambridge University Press by

White-Thomson Publishing
www.wtpub.co.uk

Editor: Sonya Newland
Designer: Clare Nicholas